In the Hands of Our Heavenly Father

A True Story of Faith, Prayer, and Miraculous
Healing from Stage IV Cancer

Daniel Zebarth

Spirit Media Publishing

Spirit Media Publishing and its logos are trademarks of Spirit Media Publishing

www.spiritmediapublishing.com

205 S Academy Street #3251
Cary, NC 27519

Religion | Christian Life | Inspirational

Paperback ISBN: 979-8-89307-222-8
eBook ISBN: 979-8-89307-216-7
PDF ISBN: 979-8-89307-217-4
Library of Congress Control Number: 2026902259

CONTENTS

BEFORE YOU BEGIN

This book began as a personal testimony written for my family, a record of God's faithfulness during my journey through cancer. Friends who walked alongside us encouraged me to share it more broadly, in the hope that others facing illness might find comfort, perspective, and faith along their own journey.

MEDICAL DISCLAIMER

This book is not intended as medical advice. The author's experience is personal and unique. Readers should consult qualified medical professionals before making healthcare decisions. Medical treatment decisions should never be made based solely on personal stories or spiritual testimony.

FAITH & TESTIMONY STATEMENT

This story reflects my personal experience with faith, prayer, medical treatment, and healing. I do not believe healing follows a formula or that faith guarantees a specific outcome. God's work in our lives is personal, sovereign, and often mysterious.

FOREWORD

In a world often dominated by skepticism or "scientific certainty," stories of profound faith and inexplicable miracles remind us that there is more to life than what meets the eye, or the microscope. *In the Hands of Our Heavenly Father* is one such story, a raw and compelling testament to the power of prayer, the resilience of the human spirit, and the boundless grace of God.

Dan's narrative begins like so many others: a routine checkup that spirals into a devastating diagnosis of pancreatic cancer in 2009. Pancreatic cancer, as Dan unflinchingly details, is one of the deadliest forms, with survival rates that plummet dramatically once it metastasizes. The statistics he shares, over 66,000 Americans diagnosed annually and a mortality rate hovering near 78 percent, paint a grim picture. Yet this book is not a tale of despair; it is a beacon of hope.

What sets this story apart is Dan's unshakable faith. Raised in a Christian home, with a life marked by service, entrepreneurship, and devotion to family, Dan had long trusted in God's plan. Facing a terminal illness tested that faith to its core. He grapples openly with questions like *How long do I have?* and *Why me?* Yet amid the pain, moments of divine intervention emerge. Dan recounts a vivid visitation from Jesus during a hospital stay, an encounter that infused him with peace and purpose. What doctors deemed impossible became reality.

Throughout the book, Dan weaves together reflections on Scripture, personal insights, and medical realities. He does not shy away from the science, yet he consistently elevates the story to the spiritual realm. His journey echoes biblical truth: *"The Lord your God is with you, the Mighty Warrior who saves."* (Zephaniah 3:17)

As you turn these pages, you will find more than a medical memoir. You will discover encouragement for your own trials. Dan's recovery, now more than a decade and a half strong, stands as a living testimony that when we place our lives in God's hands, even the darkest valleys can lead to unimaginable light.

George Pardos
A grateful friend of more than four decades

ACKNOWLEDGEMENTS

I want to especially thank my family and others who encouraged and helped me recall events when writing this book. Thank you to my wife, Kay, who read many of my drafts, continually offered encouragement, and shared her own experiences in Part IV of the book. I am also grateful to George Pardos, MD, who provided thoughtful feedback on an early version, and to Charlotte, my grandniece, who contributed her professional perspective.

This book had its beginning in 2011. At the time, I had no desire to write a book and doubted that I had the ability to do so. The writing went on hold in 2012 for reasons I did not yet understand. In 2021, I felt clearly led by the Holy Spirit to finish it. This is truly His book, a testimony of miraculous healing from Stage IV pancreatic cancer.

I am simply a vessel God has used to share that He is alive, faithful, and still working miracles today.

OPENING REMARKS

I hope you find this book, my true story of healing, prayer, hope, and trusting God, helpful in some way in your own life. In 2011, I read *90 Minutes in Heaven* by Don Piper. Knowing he had written his book just two years after his accident encouraged me to believe that perhaps I, too, could write about my journey after my diagnosis.

A song that deeply resonated with me during this time speaks about imagining what it will be like to walk beside God and stand in His presence.

I love the song "I Can Only Imagine" by MercyMe released in 2001. Many of the lyrics ring true, especially as they relate to my cancer journey.

"I can only imagine what it will be like when I walk by your side... The song goes on to say... **surrounded by your glory, what will my heart feel? ...or to my knees will I fall?"** As I reflected on my cancer journey, I realized something unexpected: rather than imagining, I was living through circumstances I never could have imagined: my diagnosis, the recovery, Christ's presence, healing, and the growth of my faith and marriage.

Throughout this book, I sometimes refer to God, sometimes to Jesus, and sometimes to the Holy Spirit. I use these terms interchangeably to reflect the Holy Trinity.

PART I

EXCERPTS

Yet I am always with you; you hold me by my right hand. You guide me with your counsel, and afterward you will take me into glory. Whom have I in heaven but you? And earth has nothing I desire besides you. My flesh and my heart may fail, but God is the strength of my heart and my portion forever. (Psalm 73:23–26)

The Lord your God is with you, the Mighty Warrior who saves. (Zephaniah 3:17)

I could NOT have imagined…

I should not be here. Pancreatic cancer patients do not survive sixteen years. They do not watch their children marry, hold grandchildren, or write books about their journey. Yet here I am in 2025, cancer-free and thriving. But back in July 2009, when I received my diagnosis, my life changed, and everything that had seemed possible suddenly faded. My life shifted in an instant, and every thought was consumed by one question: *How long do I have?*

My pancreatic cancer diagnosis changed everything! I learned quickly that I needed a positive attitude about my future if I wanted to fight and survive. This journey has had its ups and some very steep downs, like a roller coaster ride; thankfully, in the end it has been more ups than downs. Along the way there were surprises I never expected, including strengthened bonds with my family. I also learned to stay focused and to accept whatever my outcome might be, which meant trusting God's plans for me, even though that outcome remained a mystery.

Pancreatic cancer (adenocarcinoma, or cancer of the exocrine cells) is often considered the deadliest form of cancer. It has an overall survival rate of about 7.5 percent after five years and is the third most common cause of cancer deaths. It is especially deadly because it often produces few symptoms and therefore is not detected early. Life expectancy is often less than one year. When the cancer metastasizes (Stage IV), it has spread from the original site to other organs, most commonly the liver, but potentially to the lungs, peritoneum, or stomach. With metastatic disease, the five-year survival rate drops to about one percent.

There is another type of pancreatic cancer called a pancreatic neuroendocrine tumor, or pNET (a cancer of the endocrine cells). This is generally considered a somewhat less deadly form of pancreatic cancer. It is also called an islet cell tumor, named after the islands of hormone-producing cells in the pancreas.

Statistics (sources include Pancreatic.org, Cancer.gov, and the National Library of Medicine):

- 67,440 Americans will be diagnosed with pancreatic cancer (adenocarcinoma)
- 51,980 Americans are expected to die from this disease this year

- Although pancreatic cancer is the 10th most commonly diagnosed cancer in the U.S., it is the third leading cause of cancer-related deaths

Statistics (American Cancer Society, 2025, regarding pNETs, plus sources above):

- Less than 2% of pancreatic cancers are pNETs, with about 1 in 100,000 people diagnosed annually

- Survival rate after surgery: median around 50% at five years

- Survival rate after metastasis to Stage IV: around 19% at five years

Statistics (Pancreatic Cancer Action Network, 2007, regarding pNETs):

- According to a population-based study, the average life expectancy after diagnosis with a metastatic pNET is 23 months

Stage I pNET cancers can progress to Stage IV quickly, sometimes in just over one year (mine progressed in about a year and a half). While exact records of the "longest" survivor are not readily available, some studies report patients with Stage IV pNET cancer living for several years, with a few documented cases exceeding a decade. Even so, the average survival rate for Stage IV remains significantly lower, with most patients living only a few years after diagnosis. With locally advanced adenocarcinoma, half of all patients die within ten months of diagnosis, and half of those whose cancer metastasizes die within six months. Yet here I am today, sixteen years later, doing well and sharing my journey with you.

"For though we live in the world, we do not wage war as the world does. The weapons we fight with are not the weapons of the world. On the contrary, they have divine power to demolish strongholds. We demolish arguments and every pretension that sets itself up against the knowledge of God, and we take captive every thought to make it obedient to Christ." (2 Corinthians 10:3-5)

I have been blessed throughout my life with visits from Jesus. During my cancer journey, He interceded and visited me, guiding me through my most trying days and nights. In 2009, when I was told that I had adenocarcinoma of the pancreas, I believed it was a death sentence. The first good news came just days later, when my diagnosis changed from a very aggressive form of cancer to a pancreatic neuroendocrine tumor. Even so, the removal of the cancer was an extremely difficult and painful procedure in the fall of 2009, and at that time I had been given just eight months to live.

I heard and saw Him as I struggled to recover, and later that same day I was miraculously able to come back twice from unconsciousness. When the cancer later spread to my liver, the Holy Spirit stood with me and promised to work on healing me.

Finally, after years of chemotherapy, God spoke to me and told me to ask my doctor whether my cancer was still present. When the biopsy was performed, the result was benign. I knew this outcome was not possible through any natural or earthly means, but only through the supernatural healing power of God.

My cancer diagnosis was particularly daunting for me, as my earliest experiences with cancer had already shaped my childhood and influenced the course of my life. Before I share the details of my cancer journey, I want to describe events from my early years and adult life that helped mold me into who I am today and prepared me to trust Him more fully. Looking back, I can see that God was already holding my hand, quietly preparing me for the battle that lay ahead.

PART II

BIOGRAPHICAL HIGHLIGHTS

Dad, Mother and My Early Life

Dad owned and operated a full-service Mobil Oil gas station and convenience store, the Flying Red Horse, in Augusta, Wisconsin. The station was right next door to our home. Dad purchased it from the previous owner and later expanded it after my oldest sister was born. He was also the sexton (caretaker) of the two cemeteries in town. Being a sexton meant mowing, clipping grass around markers, digging and closing graves, and overseeing general maintenance. I often helped him with those tasks, as did each of my sisters. Dad was elected mayor and held the position for eight years. He also served as an alderman (city councilman) at the time of his death. Like most fathers, he worked hard and spent many hours doing so.

Mother was 38 and Dad was 48 when I was born. There was a large age gap between me and my older sisters: Helen was born in 1934, Barbara in 1937, and Mary in 1938. On the day I was born,

Dad had to work at the gas station, as usual. Mother told him, "It's time, I need to go to the hospital." Dad called a good friend, Roger Hahn, a police officer (who later became a detective), and asked him to take Mother to the hospital at four in the morning. Roger drove her in his police car, sirens and lights flashing, all the way to the hospital in Eau Claire, Wisconsin, about thirty minutes away.

I was born at 9:18 a.m. on January 14, 1952. I was named Daniel Roger, with my middle name honoring Roger Hahn for driving my mother to the hospital. Years later, Roger and I became friends. I was told I was a happy surprise for both my parents, especially my father, who finally had a son after all those daughters. I was an even bigger surprise to my sisters, because they did not know Mother was pregnant until shortly before I was born.

When I was a child, Mother made sure I attended church and Sunday school. We went to the Evangelical United Brethren Church (EUB) in Augusta. My sisters nicknamed it "the Church on the Hill," and it was there that I was confirmed. My sisters told me that Grandma Zebarth took them to church because she was concerned they would not otherwise go. Helen, my oldest sister, remembers that Grandma sometimes read from a German Bible. I do not recall my mother or father praying, even at mealtimes. The only times I remember prayer at home were during visits when Helen and her family joined us for a family meal.

I attended grade school and high school in Augusta, about a mile from our home. The school housed all grades from kindergarten through high school. When I returned home from school, walking or riding my bike, I would occasionally find bullies waiting for me. They harassed, teased, and threatened me. They never did anything beyond using their words, but it must have affected me, because I still remember those times and the dread of having to face them.

Mother's main job was supporting Dad, which enabled him to work at the gas station, tend the cemeteries, and serve as mayor. Mother showed her love in many ways. Making his supper was one of them. His supper was generally meat, potatoes, and maybe a vegetable (Dad did not like most vegetables). When he came home for supper, Mother would take her turn tending the station. Generally, he ate alone, but I remember times when Dad and I ate together and talked.

In 1963, my fifth-grade year, life brought a series of events that changed everything. In March of 1963, my father died of stomach cancer at age 59, and it felt like the end of my childhood. In November of that year, the assassination of John F. Kennedy brought even more shock. During that same year, I also experienced several "firsts": my first pair of glasses and my first official job, delivering newspapers. That pivotal year taught me how quickly life can change.

I remember three things happening within a day or so after Dad died. First, I recall my mother calling me into the kitchen to tell me he had died. She explained that he would not be around anymore. I did not comprehend what that meant. I went back into the living room and resumed whatever I had been doing, trying to understand it as best I could.

Second, a day or so later, a newspaper reporter came to our home to gather information for Dad's obituary. Mother spoke with him on our enclosed front porch while I quietly listened from the next room. One of the questions he asked Mother during their conversation was if Dad had been married before or had other children. Mother hesitated and then answered that he had. That was new information to me, but I did not think much about it at the time.

Third, over the next few months, Mother sometimes asked me to sleep in her bedroom. I do not know if it comforted her to have someone nearby, or if she feared losing me too and wanted to watch over me. Helen later told me Mother was "lost" after Dad died. That may have been another reason for the request.

I was eleven when Dad died, and I had not yet gotten to know him on a personal level. I have no idea what his inner life was like: how he felt, what he feared, what stressed him, or how he dealt with his burdens. Years later, I found photographs Mother had taken during the eleven years I had with him. Those pictures paint him as a loving, caring father and man. I also learned about him from the people of Augusta, from customers on my paper route, and from stories Roger Hahn and others shared with me. Everyone genuinely liked my dad.

One of my sisters told me Dad was encouraged to run for county office after his term as mayor ended. He told them he was not interested. He was not a political person and he was not swayed by others who tried to tell him what to do or how to vote. He simply wanted what was best for the town.

My sister Barbara later shared that in the fall of 1962 Dad and I drove to visit her near Milwaukee, Wisconsin, where she lived. I was not allowed inside because her children had measles, but Dad visited with her. During that visit, he told Barbara he was not well and asked her to keep a secret: he had a daughter, Evelyn, from a previous marriage. He told Barbara she should share that news with her siblings when the time was right.

Years later, Barbara shared this news just as Dad had asked. Evelyn and I became friends, and over time we grew close and communicated regularly. She was twenty-five when I was born. I organized a family reunion in 1992 at Winter Park, Colorado, and I made sure Evelyn and her family were invited. They came to the reunion which gave all of us the opportunity to become acquainted. Uncle Herb, the patriarch, shared memories of my dad and of their early years. He was the hit of the reunion and did a wonderful job telling stories.

I was very proud of my dad. I looked up to him. It must have been hard for him to share that secret with Barbara. I believe he knew he was nearing the end of his life. I am glad he shared it, because otherwise I would never have known Evelyn and her family. Looking back, I believe God was organizing all of that so Evelyn could become part of my life. Perhaps, in some way, it also influenced me to be more open and share more about myself, as I have in this book. I believe it strengthened me in many ways.

One special moment with Dad was captured in a photo Mother took. I was four years old, and Dad was holding me in his arms in front of a large rock formation, probably near Wisconsin Dells. My father instilled three things in me: a strong work ethic, the importance of learning many skills, and the determination to push through life's challenges. Barbara once told me Dad smoked cigarettes for many years, then got very sick one time and quit cold turkey. Dad set an example for me by working hard, and he did it with a smile.

The Gas Station

About three months before Dad's death, he signed a one-year lease with someone to operate the gas station. I assume he knew he was very sick. The lease went into effect in December 1962. Near the end of that lease, Mother told me the man was not doing a good job. Years later, I found the newspaper clipping Mother saved, advertising for his replacement. She never found anyone, so Mother and I took on the operation of the station ourselves. I was about twelve years old.

For about three and one half years, Mother and I ran the station. Mother worked there during the hours I was in school. I usually opened the station in the morning, went to school, then returned to work until we closed in the evening. I did homework during slow periods.

Running a station in the late 1960s meant greeting customers, filling gas tanks (there was no self-service then), checking oil, cleaning windows, and making sure we were paid. It also meant stocking grocery items, because we sold milk, homemade ice cream sandwiches (which Mother made), candy, snacks, and similar items. After closing, I balanced the register, updated the manual ledgers, and placed orders for gasoline and other supplies.

Working at the station meant I did not have much time for school events or time with friends outside of school, but I do not recall being resentful. I believed my duty was to help Mother and keep the station running. Looking back, it was a good life lesson and a valuable experience. I know it shaped me and helped mold me into who I am. My mentors were Dad, Mother, my sisters, and later my Uncle Herb.

Living alone with Mother was difficult at times. She did not openly express love and rarely hugged anyone. This was especially true toward my sisters' husbands, and sometimes toward people in general. Mother often reinterpreted what others said in ways they did not intend, and it distressed her and affected her mood. After Dad died, no one could soften her feelings when she was hurt.

I know this also affected me. Over time, it may have made me more accepting of others, partly because Mother was not. I also learned quickly that Mother was deeply afraid of the Internal Revenue Service (IRS). She worried they would shut down the station due to imperfect records or that they would audit the business. Those fears upset me. The government, or any agency, should not be able to intimidate small business owners so easily. It bothered me that she lived with that fear.

In hindsight, I know that fear influenced my decision to go into accounting and later pursue becoming a Certified Public Accountant (CPA). I wanted to protect Mother and other small business owners like her, from that fear.

Recollections and Memories

There was a thirteen-year gap between me and my youngest sister, Mary. In many ways, I was like an only child. I have been told that Mary was Dad's pride and joy. She was a bit of a tomboy and Dad called her Sammie. When I came along, that changed.

I do not know my parents' faith or beliefs with certainty. I do believe God was part of their lives, minds, and hearts, even though they did not attend church regularly. I believe this because of the values they demonstrated and what I later learned about them from others. They attended Christmas and Easter services, and Mother made sure I attended church regularly and completed confirmation classes.

I did not read books as a child, even though I spent a lot of time alone. I entertained myself with a big sandpile and my Tonka trucks. I built things with Tinkertoys and with my American Brick set. My best friend was my nephew, Greg Sieg who lived about ten miles away. Greg and I played together often.

My sisters each remember attending EUB camp, led by my uncle, Reverend Herb Zebarth, with his wife, Aunt Meta, serving as the camp nurse. When it was my turn to attend camp, Uncle Herb had become pastor of a Methodist church; later he became district super-intendent for the Methodist churches in Wisconsin. I admired and respected Uncle Herb, Dad's youngest brother. He was calm and thoughtful and seemed to have answers to many of my life questions. Later in life, I came to view him as a father figure. I am sure some of his faith rubbed off on me.

Uncle Herb and I became even closer after Mother's death, and closer still after I married Kay. As Uncle Herb was nearing the end of his life, I remember him saying, "Lord, I hope I have been good and faithful enough." I loved my Uncle Herb.

Mother taught me a bedtime prayer that she made sure I said every night while kneeling beside my bed: "Now I lay me down to sleep, I pray the Lord my soul to keep; if I shall die before I wake, I pray the Lord my soul to take." This traditional prayer originated in the eighteenth century. The words "if I shall die before I wake" seemed strange for a young child to say, but I did not think much about it at the time.

It is hard to believe that Mother did not have a driver's license when Dad died. She struggled with the driving portion of the test and took it many times. She grew very frustrated. My brother-in-law, Gordon, offered to help her practice driving, and he took her out repeatedly so she could become more confident. Gordon was likely her least favorite son-in-law, yet he was an immense help. God has a sense of humor in putting two people together like that.

The Move to Pecatonica

During 1966–1967, my ninth-grade year at Augusta High School, Mother found a buyer for our house and the station. In the summer of 1967, we moved to Pecatonica, Illinois. Mother had siblings in that area, and I am certain she was grateful for their company and support. It was a relief to have the burden of the station off our backs, but it was also a tough move, and an incredibly challenging one for me. I was leaving behind friends I had known all my life.

We lived with my mother's oldest brother, Ed, in a two-story home with a large front porch, and I have many good memories from that time. In 1968, Mother purchased a home close to the high school. When I graduated, she organized a graduation party at our home. This is a special memory because Mother did not enjoy organizing events, and I know she put a fair amount of time and effort into making it happen.

As an upperclassman in high school, I knew I needed to participate in extracurricular activities to improve my chances of being accepted into college. I chose to run the two-mile track and the two-and-a-half-mile cross-country race, partly because they were non-contact sports. I did well in school and made the honor roll, but not without a lot of study and hard work. I also had a couple of jobs while living in Pecatonica. One was working at Mary & Dave's fruit and vegetable farm in Stillman Valley. They grew corn, melons, strawberries, and tomatoes, which we delivered to local grocery stores in and around Rockford, Illinois. I also worked part-time at Dean's

Foods, starting in 1969. I was laid off in June 1970, right after my high school graduation.

During my senior year, I met with my high school counselor and told him I was interested in accounting. He said I needed to go away to school rather than attend a local junior or community college, which had been my plan. I explained that my mother would not do well if I left the area. Also, I did not qualify for most four-year colleges because I had only one year of a foreign language. The move from Augusta to Pecatonica created this complication: Augusta offered Spanish, while Pecatonica High School offered French.

I applied to a couple of colleges sight unseen. My counselor recommended the University of Illinois (U of I) in Champaign, and I agreed without much thought. He worked his magic, and I was accepted after an initial rejection. My acceptance was conditional, requiring me to complete a second year of Spanish in college—which, interestingly, I was never actually required to do. I also had an advantage because our bookkeeping teacher at Pecatonica received permission from Illinois State College to offer a college-level accounting class to select students. The class counted for three college credits. I took it and never looked back. My goal of becoming an accounting major and a CPA had officially begun. I was also fortunate to earn a small scholarship from Pecatonica High School. (God is great, although I did not realize it then. He was holding my hand and guiding me.)

College was still two months away when I was laid off from my factory job and suddenly had extra time on my hands. Barbara and her family had moved to Brussels, Belgium, in 1969. I found myself thinking that Mother and I should go visit her (the Holy Spirit, talking to me). I had saved several thousand dollars for college from various jobs. I shared the idea with Mother and told her I could pay for the trip with some of that money, and she could repay me later. So off we went, on a three-week trip to Belgium in August 1970.

We saw and did so much while staying with my sister and her family. Ed, Barbara's husband, served as our tour guide. We traveled to Belgium, Paris, Venice, several cities in Germany, and Luxembourg, to name a few. Ed was a history buff and shared many facts and details about each place we visited. Barbara later told me that during our time in Europe, she and Mother had special talks and shared meaningful memories.

That trip was, and will always be, a special memory. I am so glad I was able to make it happen. God placed the idea in my head. Looking back, it is hard to believe how perfectly everything had to line up for that trip to happen, getting passports, purchasing tickets at the right time, and coordinating all the details. That trip had a huge impact on me, and it still does. I learned that I truly love helping others when it is within my ability.

College

After returning from Europe, I headed to the University of Illinois. I quickly realized my counselor had made the right recommendation for me. I studied hard just to earn B's my first year. I came home for Christmas in 1970, and when it was time to return to college, Mother begged me not to go back. She cried and cried, but I knew I had to return, even with that huge emotional challenge. To this day, I do not know what gave me the strength to leave my mother behind and go back to school. (It had to be God's hand.)

The following Christmas break in 1971, Mother appeared very weak. After I returned to college, I learned from my sister Mary, who lived near Mother in Prairieville, Illinois, that she had been caring for her at home. Mother could not have been there more than two weeks, because I had just seen her over Christmas break. She deteriorated quickly. Mother called me on January 14, 1972, to wish me a happy twentieth birthday. She sounded so very weak. Three days later, I received a call from Mary telling me Mother had died. She suffered a massive pulmonary embolism from a blood clot in her legs. This was about seventeen months after our August 1970 trip to Brussels. Mother had wanted to repay me for the trip but was never able to. For me, that was a blessing. It was the greatest gift I had ever given my mother.

Her death came at the start of semester finals. I rescheduled my exams and returned one week later to complete them. The professors were accommodating. However, there was one final I did not do well on—Cost Accounting. The professor called me in, talked with me about it, and suggested I consider changing majors. I thought for a brief moment and replied, "No." Looking back, I know his words were not meant to be unkind; his intentions were probably good. Still, I could have accepted his advice and followed his suggestion, and I cannot imagine how dramatically different my life would be today.

Mother's death was very hard. In a sense, I was truly on my own, as all my sisters lived far away and had left home years earlier. I was sad to lose my mother, but in another sense her death helped me focus even harder on finishing college. It freed me from constantly worrying about how she was doing at home, alone. From the end of my sophomore year through graduation, I had a single focus, college. My grades improved, and studying became easier.

At the end of my junior year, I moved out of the dorm (the dorms were closed during the summer) and took a summer class so my senior year could be even more focused on passing the CPA exam. During my college years I also worked various jobs to support myself through college, including working at a gas station, driving a taxi, and working at a car wash. During my senior year, I worked as a bookkeeper at a nursing home, my first job in the healthcare field. I simply did what I had to do to accomplish the goals I had set many years before. Behind the scenes was God, though little did I know it then.

During part of my junior and senior years, I had a girlfriend, but her mother forced us to break up. After the breakup, I received a call from a local social services agency telling me she was pregnant, about three months before the child was born. I had not known, and my former girlfriend had never told me. I received another call in March, shortly after the birth. The agency said the child was a healthy boy and that he was immediately adopted by a family. I never heard anything from the boy's mother again. I worried that I would be asked to pay support or provide financial assistance, but that never happened.

At the end of my senior year, it was time to take the CPA exam. Approximately 21 percent pass the test on the first attempt. It is long and extensive; the time allotted was nineteen and one-half hours, spread over two and one-half days. I took the exam in early May. Two weeks later, on May 19, 1974, I graduated from college. Three months after that, I received a letter stating that I had passed the CPA exam. I had worked hard, and I was ready for my career.

First Job, Marriage and Divorce

My first job was with McGladrey Hansen and Dunn in Iowa City, Iowa, earning a salary of $11,000 in 1974. I was a staff accountant, worked on audits, and prepared tax returns. After about three years, I decided public accounting was not the career path I wanted. Long hours were expected to please the partners, and they worked even longer. My long-term plan was not to be glued to my work. Even so,

I learned a great deal during those three years, basic skills that prepared me for every job I would hold in the future.

I met Karen in Iowa City in the fall of 1974, and our relationship grew quickly. Karen had two boys, Don and Brian, from her previous marriage; they were four and seven at the time. I genuinely felt sorry for them because their father was hardly involved in their lives. Karen and I married in September 1975, and in September 1976, at the one-year mark, as Iowa required, I legally adopted Don and Brian. I had decided early in our relationship that I would adopt them as soon as I could. Karen's ex-husband agreed to sign his parental rights over to me, which was required for the adoption. It still surprises me how easily he gave up those rights.

I accepted a job in Sioux City, Iowa, at Postal Finance, a large national loan company. Karen, the boys, and I relocated there. We rented an apartment at first and later bought a house. I became involved with the local Optimist Club. A friend encouraged me to run for president. I reluctantly agreed, and I won. Their motto was "Friend of Youth." That meant we worked with youth, giving them opportunities they might not otherwise have had. We camped and spent time together, which was a blessing, though at the time I did not fully appreciate it because I was still very introspective. Some of my best memories are spending time with the club's older members and learning about their lives, experiences, and challenges.

At Postal Finance, I learned about bureaucracy, how layers of management can put stress on employees and make meaningful change difficult. In 1980, I changed jobs and went to work for FEH Associates, an architectural and design firm, as their controller. It was a smaller company of twenty to thirty employees, and I realized I liked that environment better. One of my goals was to take the best of what I had seen in each job and adopt those best practices for myself, using those skills whenever possible, whether in business or in personal life. I was also fortunate to form a lifelong friendship with Neil, a coworker at FEH. He and I have remained friends through many hardships and shared challenges.

Karen, the boys, and I did many things as a family and made many good memories together. We regularly went to church, traveled for vacations, and had many family adventures. However, our marriage was becoming a challenge for me. I believed the boys should be disciplined one way, and Karen believed they needed another approach. I was trying to tell her how to be a good mother, yet I had no real idea how to raise children myself.

After four years of marriage, I found myself struggling and wondering whether I should remain married. I learned quickly how painful that decision could be. To marry someone and step immediately into a ready-made family was not easy, and I was not prepared for it. I agonized over it in my mind and heart for about a year. I was young and selfish, and in hindsight I can see how much my focus was on me. I felt terrible for Don and Brian, now thirteen and ten, because they were going to lose another father.

I prayed, and I continued to pray, asking what I should do, while constantly questioning whether I should pursue a divorce. It was a trying time, emotionally and mentally. What made it even harder was that I had been raised to believe a marriage before God was permanent. On so many levels, I believed divorce was wrong. Yet neither Karen nor I was happy in our strained relationship, and one or both of us would have needed to make major changes for the marriage to work.

I moved out of our home a couple of times. Once I stayed in a cheap hotel for about a week. Another time, I lived in a rental house I owned that happened to be vacant. I stayed there while battling with the decision. I hoped that time alone would bring clarity and help me reflect on what I should do and what would be best.

One distinct night, as I lay on the floor in my sleeping bag, weeping and agonizing over that major decision, Jesus appeared.

Jesus stood at my feet, small in stature. He said, "I know that you are struggling with your decision. It is okay to move on." No one knew my emotional struggle. I had not shared my agony with anyone, not even my spouse. After He spoke, He quickly left.

How did I know it was Jesus? For several reasons:

1. He looked like the biblical descriptions: medium-length hair, a beard, and Hebrew clothing, including a simla with tallits on the corners.

2. He was very small, standing near my feet. It seemed He was less than two feet tall, and yet He looked normal—fully adult.

3. I am sure no one else could have heard His words, even if someone had been present.

4. He came and went very quickly, with no visible entrance or departure.

I did not know what to think. I wondered, Was this real? It was my first personal encounter like this, and no one, not even my Uncle Reverend Herb, had ever told me that Jesus might appear or visit us. I was confused about how to process it, yet I knew I needed Him. I had been calling out for help. It was hard to comprehend, but God knew my deep emotional struggle that night.

I believe this kind of miracle should not surprise us when we read the Bible. Scripture says, *"Ask and it will be given to you; seek and you will find; knock and the door will be opened to you"* (Matthew 7:7). And

Revelation 3:20 says, *"Here I am! I stand at the door and knock. If anyone hears my voice and opens the door, I will come in and eat with that person, and they with me."* I called out to Him in one of my greatest times of need. I heard His voice and welcomed Him in to help me.

What an incredible event. Its perfect timing was overwhelming then, and it still is today. I remained in my sleeping bag and eventually fell asleep. In the days that followed, I thought a lot about His visit and carefully considered His words. God does not condone divorce, and at the time I was not even sure divorce was what I wanted. Yet I also believe everything happens for a reason and has a purpose. Days turned into weeks as I continued to process what He had said. It took a long time to realize that, in a way, I believe He was giving me permission to do what I was struggling to accept.

At that time, my faith was strong enough to lean on in difficult moments, but it was not especially deep or powerful. Jesus' visit began a season of growth. Slowly, my faith grew after that astonishing event. One might expect leaps and bounds. Yet, I occasionally still wondered if the visit had been real. I am thankful that God intervenes in our lives, especially as He did in 1980 with that visit. For me, it began a long journey, sometimes slow, toward trusting Him with everything. My faith strengthened and I became a more faithful follower of Christ. Some would call this being "born again," meaning a person who has experienced spiritual rebirth and has come to have a personal relationship with Jesus Christ. Jesus' visit profoundly changed me. I know God loves us and wants to bless us, but this was the first time I became aware that He might personally visit or speak to us.

When I reflect now, I believe I interpreted His message correctly. In 1981, at the time of our divorce, I could not have known what 2009 would bring, when both Karen and I would face cancer diagnoses. Had we remained married, caring for each other through such trials would have been extremely difficult, perhaps impossible. God saw what was coming and directed each of us down a necessary path. Divorce was not His ideal, but I believe His message to me was one of understanding. I have received His forgiveness for that decision, yet at times I still ask myself, *What if we had stayed together?*

I attended Karen's memorial service in November 2023. I was anxious, not knowing how her siblings might receive me because of our divorce. Her family was welcoming. We talked, shared many stories, and discovered we had a lot in common. We got along very well. That was not at all what I expected. God is so good, all the time.

I later asked Brian and Don what their mother said to them after our divorce. Brian said she was fairly quiet about it. She might say things like, "We haven't been getting along," or, "Sometimes people fall apart," but she did not speak much about it. Karen could have spoken negatively about me, but she chose not to. I am truly thankful for that. My regret is that I knew Karen was quite ill, yet I did not call, send a card, or reach out personally to express how sorry I was for her health challenges. I regularly asked Don and Brian how she was doing, but I should have contacted her myself before she passed.

After the divorce, in early 1981, I accepted a controller position with a real estate development and construction company in Fullerton, California, and relocated there. The move allowed me to be closer to my sister Barbara and her family. Don and Brian remained in Sioux City, which was difficult, but I felt it was necessary in order to move forward. That job taught me about business relationships, how to work successfully with investors, and even how to dress depending on whom I was meeting. The move also gave me a fresh start.

Kay, California and Colorado

I met Kay while working in Sioux City, before I made the decision to move to California. We worked at the same company, and I would walk by her work area so I could talk to her. After asking her out several times, she finally agreed. We continued to date even after I moved to California, which was especially challenging. Despite the distance, we were committed to each other, and the rest is history.

Her parents welcomed me with cinnamon rolls every time I visited, but her father also made it clear he was watching closely and wanted no harm or unhappiness to come into his daughter's life. I assume every father wants the best for his daughter, and I was largely unknown to him. After several months of dating, Kay and I got engaged.

Looking back, the story of our marriage is remarkable. Kay and I thought we had everything under control. We planned a small ceremony on her parents' farm in Iowa in July 1982. I arrived on Thursday evening. On Friday, the day before the wedding, we went to the Sioux City courthouse to get our marriage license. The clerk asked how she could help, and we told her we needed a marriage license. She asked for our blood tests, which we did not have, and we did not even know we needed. She said, "You can come back for your license once you have those tests, which generally takes a couple of days."

We explained that our wedding was the next day and that the minister, family, and friends were already coming. To us, everything suddenly felt like it was in jeopardy. We asked the clerk what options we had. She suggested that South Dakota had different rules and that we could try there.

We immediately drove forty minutes to Vermillion, South Dakota, the county seat. We went in to get a license, and during casual conversation the clerk asked where we were getting married. We excitedly answered, "Sioux City, Iowa." She informed us that a South Dakota marriage license was valid only in South Dakota.

Now what were we going to do? We asked if there were any other options. She pleasantly replied that we would have to get married in South Dakota, and that a Justice of the Peace was available and could marry us right away. We had run out of other choices. Kay and I agreed to get married at the courthouse.

We were taken to a room, and shortly after, an older lady came in to preside. Two witnesses were secured, as required. As the justice spoke, she gently swayed from side to side, a fond memory now. That was Friday, July 9. Kay and I decided not to tell anyone about our "actual" wedding day, because we knew it would change how our guests viewed the Saturday ceremony.

That night we slept in separate bedrooms at her parents' house. No surprise, this was not how we had planned our wedding-night celebration. Outside Kay's bedroom window stood a maple tree, under whose branches we would be married by a pastor, with God's blessings, on her parent's farm on Saturday. In a sense, we were married twice: Friday in South Dakota and Saturday in Iowa. To this day, we celebrate both days as anniversaries. One could say we have celebrated eighty-four times instead of forty-two, at least as of 2025.

The day after our Saturday wedding, we began our life journey together. We started in a van full of Kay's belongings, headed to California. We lived in an apartment managed by my employer for less than a year before we began talking about buying a home. But California home prices were completely unaffordable. Our research showed we would have to live at least an hour away from our jobs to afford a house. After many discussions, we decided to leave California.

Now we had to decide where to go. Colorado was an option because it was roughly midway between our families. We studied the Colorado Front Range area. I had previously traveled to Denver for a few interviews, with no success. But we felt that if we actually lived in Denver, my job prospects would be improved.

In May 1983, we gave notice to our employers and our landlord. With no jobs secured but some cash saved, we took a huge leap of faith and drove to Colorado in a U-Haul loaded with our belongings, towing our car behind. I had an interview scheduled the next day with Beaumont Properties. The day after that interview, I received an offer to be their corporate controller, and it included a company car. God is good. Kay found a job a few days later with AmeriGas.

With jobs secured, we moved into an apartment in Lakewood, Colorado. After living there for close to six months, we purchased our first home together on South Simms Street in Littleton, Colorado. God, again, was right there in the details.

About a year later I was laid off. It was a real struggle to find a new job, but I eventually secured a position with Denver Clinic Medical Centers (Accord) near downtown Denver as their Chief Financial Officer. This job was a godsend in more ways than one, because it allowed me to meet people who would later support me through troubling times when medical concerns arose. During my time at Accord, I met George Pardos, MD and I also earned an MBA from the University of Phoenix.

Our Family

Kay and I owned our first home for close to three years. We decided to look for a larger home, and in November 1986 we purchased the house we still live in today. As of this writing in 2025, we have lived in our home for thirty-nine years. It was a big stretch of our budget, but our income grew, and over time we became very comfortable in our new home.

Our first son, Isaac, was born in November 1988. He was born with serious, life-threatening health challenges caused by a prolapsed umbilical cord, which led to a lack of oxygen during his birth. The prolapse happened while we were on our way to the hospital. Isaac was born at Presbyterian/St. Luke's Hospital in Denver after an emergency delivery. A few days later, the doctors recommended that we transfer him to Children's Hospital, where he could receive the specialized care he needed. At Children's Hospital, he was stabilized and grew stronger. He remained in the hospital for about a month. During that time, Isaac was diagnosed with spastic cerebral palsy (CP).

Isaac brought so much joy to our lives, but it was heartbreaking to realize how little he could do on his own. We were blessed that our health insurance helped with the care he needed at home, including physical therapy, respiratory therapy, occupational therapy, and speech. Life changed so quickly, from being pregnant, to suddenly having a son who required regular and intensive care. I continued to work, and Kay did as well. Having health insurance was a priority for us with Isaac's health challenges. Pre-existing conditions would disqualify a family from health insurance in those years. If either of us lost our job, at least the other would still have insurance coverage for Isaac. We were blessed with three dedicated, loving healthcare providers who came to our home and cared for Isaac while we worked. Looking back on those months now, I don't know how we managed. Life was very stressful; we took it one day at a time—and we prayed.

Isaac lived for nine months before his small body gave out. Just a few days before his death, we were holding Isaac in our arms when he looked at us and smiled. He had not smiled before. We will never forget that precious moment. We also have a special picture of Kay holding Isaac in her arms, taken by her sister. When the film was developed, one of the photos had captured light rays shining down upon their faces. This scene had occurred only days before Isaac's passing. It was a moment of great comfort...and awe, when we saw the photo. It was as if God was telling us, through that photograph, that He loved us, that He loved Isaac, and that He was watching over him. Kay has always loved photography. God spoke to her through that photograph, to her heart and to her grief for Isaac, in a way so specific and significant. We called them "Angel Rays." We knew it was a sign from God that He loved us and that He would take good care of our Isaac.

Isaac passed away in late August 1989 and is buried in Sioux City, Iowa. After Isaac's death, we held a fundraiser and helped build a new playground dedicated to him at Heritage United Methodist Church. During that time, we got to know Tom and Sue, friends who had also experienced the loss of a son around the same time. We were walking through similar life challenges, and we found support in each other. We were able to talk honestly about our grief and our trying days.

Did Isaac's health challenges and his death affect our faith? Someone could ask, "How can you still believe in a God who would allow this to happen?" For many, this would be a major challenge to their faith. We were deeply impacted emotionally, and we were heartbroken over our loss—how could we not be? Speaking for myself, Isaac actually brought us closer to God. Our trust and hope in Him grew a great deal during those years.

We wonder how anyone without faith, or without trust in God, can make it through a tragedy like the loss of a child. Every one of us has hard times in life. Without God, Kay and I cannot understand how anyone could endure such a loss. We believe Isaac is in heaven, jumping and running, something he would never have been able to do on earth. God held our hands through that awful struggle. He strengthened us, and He strengthened our faith. This became the beginning of a new chapter in our faith journey. We drew closer to God and trusted Him more as the years passed. You never fully recover from losing a child.

Now, thirty-seven years later (2025), we still mourn the loss of Isaac. Every year on his birthday, we release balloons and watch them float upwards to his heavenly home. We await the day when we will see him again and be reunited.

We started attending Heritage United Methodist Church in 1989. Over time, we attended regularly and became more involved with our new church family. I had visited a few times prior to Isaac's birth. Isaac was baptized by Reverend Brown, who agreed to baptize him in our home. Later, I became the church treasurer and held that role for fifteen years. Kay joined the handbell choir and taught in Sunday school ministries.

We waited some time before we began to grow our family again. Later, we were blessed with two more children.

Our son Zachary was born in December 1990. He was active in Cub Scouts and Boy Scouts and earned his Eagle Scout. He trained in Tae Kwon Do, led some classes, and achieved his second-degree black belt before retiring from the sport. Zach was in the talented-and-gifted program during elementary and middle school and went through the

International Baccalaureate program in high school. He attended the University of Colorado at Boulder and graduated in 2011 with a degree in Integrative Physiology. Next, he attended medical school at the University of Illinois in Chicago, where he earned his Doctor of Physical Therapy. Zach married his wife, Sarah, in October 2023, and they have a home in Arvada, Colorado. Zach is a director with a physical therapy group that is closely aligned with Panorama Orthopedics in Golden. Sarah is an assistant principal and a coach for other math teachers at a middle school in Denver.

Daisy was born in February 1993. When she was 11, she discovered Westernaires, a horse-riding organization whose motto is "precision drill riding at speed." She got her first horse, Sequel, and rode him most of the time during her years in the program. She was active with Westernaires for eight years and graduated from Precisionettes. She also rode with the Evergreen Riding Club and later with a mounted shooting team. Daisy attended D'Evelyn High School, known for its rigorous academic program. After graduation, she attended Metropolitan State University and earned a degree in Biology with a minor in Chemistry. Later, she obtained certificates as an X-ray technician and a CT technologist.

Daisy married Jeff in October 2018, exactly five years to the day before her brother's wedding. Daisy and Jeff have a home on ten acres in Elizabeth, Colorado, where they keep many animals: chickens, ducks, goats, cows, a horse, donkeys, pigs, and of course dogs and cats. Daisy is a lead CT technologist at an Adventist hospital in Littleton, Colorado. Jeff is a lead optometric technician for an ophthalmology and optometric practice in Castle Rock. When Daisy was born, two-year old Zachary started saying, "Daddy Daisy Mommy," which meant, "Give Daisy to Daddy so I can have Mommy to myself."

After Zach's birth, I felt it was time to begin searching for my biological son, who had been born shortly before I graduated college in 1974. Through a lot of research, phone calls, and letters to agencies near Champaign, Illinois, I eventually found the placement agency. They helped put us in contact, and after a call or two, we arranged our first meeting. We agreed to meet at a hotel near Denver International Airport in 1993. His first question to me was difficult, but easy to answer: "Why did you abandon me?" I explained what had happened and that I had no say in that decision.

It was difficult to explain to Zach and Daisy, when they were young, how Bill, Brian, and Don were related to them. It can be hard to be honest without sharing every detail. Kay graciously accepted Bill, Don, and Brian as if they were her own children. I am so grateful for her kindness and her attitude toward them. It has been a blessing to be involved in their lives and in the lives of their children—our grandchildren. I truly love and enjoy the times we are together.

My three children do not live near us. Bill, now living in Iowa, got married when Zachary and Daisy were still young. He often came to stay with us at Christmas for a few days, and he enjoyed interacting and playing with them. Brian moved to Colorado, so he was much more available and even lived with us for a few months. Later, Brian moved to Florida. Don has always lived in Sioux City and would come to Colorado about once a year, staying for a week or so. All the children seemed to get along and enjoy each other's company. As we have all grown older, and as everyone has built their own lives, the interactions are less frequent. Still, it is so special that Kay warmly accepts and welcomes them whenever they visit, or whenever we go to see them. All of them are truly part of our family.

Starting My Companies

As part of my job search in mid-1992, after being laid off from Accord, I reached out to many colleagues, friends, and other associates. One day, while visiting with Leigh, a new idea was planted. Leigh had been Accord's marketing consultant, and she encouraged me to start my own business. *No way,* I thought. I had financial obligations, Zach was almost two, and we were expecting a new baby. Yet my job search was not producing results. After some time passed, I began to think seriously about starting my own firm.

George Pardos, who had become both a friend and coworker while we were at Accord, was essential to my plan. He had left Accord Medical Centers two years earlier and started his own company, Omni Eye Specialists, and his business was growing and doing well. I contacted him and asked, "If I start my own CPA business, would you be a client?" He told me there was an 80 percent chance he would be. I know God was holding my hand again during this stressful period. (George wrote the foreword to this book, for which I am extremely grateful.) Even with George's reassuring answer, starting my own business was still scary. But in September 1992, I started my CPA firm. For several years I worked from home, until the firm outgrew my small office space.

George did become my first client, but that was not all. Accord contacted me in mid-September and asked if I would come back to help them. That became my second client. I also reached out to a consultant who had worked with us at Accord. He had a client in Peoria, Illinois, implementing a new system, and he asked if I wanted to help. Now I had three clients. I traveled to Peoria almost every week. From that point forward, the firm grew. Leigh and Gary, marketing consultants, also became clients.

As my business expanded, I needed more help than Kay could reasonably provide. In late 1996, I hired a full-time CPA to assist and help grow the firm. He later became a part-owner of the company.

With that addition, and with my new CPA's help, we continued to grow Zebarth Advisors into a respectable-size firm. Leigh helped us create the "Think Ahead" logo, and we decided it was important to register it as a trademark. In June 2002, we passed the required tests to become licensed to sell insurance, investments, and related advisory services, and we formed Zebarth Capital Group.

From my first job after college, I learned that I did not want to work long hours. Yet now I found myself, especially in "tax season", working eighty-hour weeks for at least a few weeks each year. Still, working long hours for yourself is different from working long hours for someone else, and it helps when you love what you do. As Zebarth Advisors continued to grow, I was no longer able to spend as much time personally connecting with clients. I missed that time and those relationships. I enjoy helping others, and through my firms I was able to do just that, helping people with business, financial, and personal challenges.

The growing success of my businesses allowed me to help my clients and support my family. I have helped many businesses with financial challenges, from the basics of recordkeeping and payroll processing to minimizing tax burdens in legal and responsible ways.

Our family has been blessed with many wonderful vacations, including cruises, skiing, road trips to see family, and other distant places we traveled together. God has been so, so good.

PART III

Cancer, My Journey

- CHAPTER 1 -
PREPARING FOR THE BIG NEWS

Career Changes – Selling My Firms

By 2009, I was 57 years old. I had built a successful life: a thriving business, a marriage, and children I adored. I had survived my parents' early deaths, a painful divorce, and the loss of our infant son. I thought I had faced the worst life could throw at me.

I was wrong.

I was about to be ambushed by one of the deadliest forms of cancer. Thankfully, the career changes I made the year before my diagnosis helped me survive what came next. I was blessed, because behind the scenes God was already involved. He had nudged me to sell my firms and accept a job that offered superior health insurance.

My new employer's health insurance plan likely saved me about $75,000 because the Mayo Clinic was in-network. Under the coverage

I had with my own firm, Mayo would have been out-of-network, and I would have paid the typical thirty percent co-insurance for out-of-network doctors and hospitals. That new insurance gave me access to excellent doctors and facilities that I likely would not have used, or could not have afforded, if I had not accepted that job offer. Let me explain how God was involved in my transition from selling my companies to securing that new role.

Omni Eye Specialists and George Pardos MD, was my largest client at Zebarth Advisors. He started his business in late 1989, and it grew into Madison Street Companies (MSC), an integrated medical organization focused on ophthalmology and related surgeries. In the latter part of 2005, George asked to meet with me. At that meeting, he asked if I would come work for him full-time.

After giving it careful thought, I told him the timing was not right. To accept the position, I would need to sell my firms, and at that time I did not believe they were at a size or level where they could be sold. I told George it would take roughly two years to prepare my businesses for that milestone. We agreed to talk again in two years.

Two years later, the Holy Spirit was telling me the time had come. George and I met again in late fall 2007. This time, we agreed that I would come to work for him. We worked out suitable terms, and with the agreement of my partner, I began the process of selling my firms. I started my new career as MSC's Senior Vice President of Finance in January 2008.

My naïve thought at the time was, *I am selling my firms, I will make a profit, and I will put cash in the bank.* My new employer also offered better health insurance, a salary, and paid time off—benefits my growing firms could not truly afford. And then, just a year and a half after starting that new job, in July 2009, I received my official cancer diagnosis. During that journey, George, as both my boss and my friend, became an even more incredible boss and friend.

There was a transition period with my businesses, so I was not full-time with MSC until mid-2008. I thoroughly enjoyed the new role, and once again I worked long hours. I had a large staff reporting to me (around thirty people). I was an integral part of the management team and very involved as we acquired other businesses. I retired from MSC in December of 2015, and the blessings from that time have continued.

The Diagnosis of Cancer

In mid-June 2009, I had three days of unusual stomach pains. I probably would have ignored them because the pain went away quickly. But for some reason (God), I felt compelled to make certain it was nothing serious. So I scheduled an appointment with my PCP (Primary Care Physician) for June 29.

After his examination, he said, "I believe you have gallstones. I'm ordering an ultrasound to confirm."

Every year, Kay and I, along with our children, Zach and Daisy, traveled to Mitchell, South Dakota, for Kay's Fourth of July family reunion. When we returned from that year's reunion, I went in for the scheduled ultrasound of my abdomen and gallbladder on July 7th.

When I think back on that exam, I remember the ultrasound technologist telling the other technologist to re-scan that area. I didn't know what that meant at the time, but later I realized she had seen something concerning and wanted it scanned again. The mass on my pancreas measured 2.8 x 2.9 x 3.3 cm on the head of the pancreas, about the size of a large grape.

My PCP called me the next day with the results. I knew something was wrong because normally his nurse would call with lab or test results. He told me the ultrasound showed a mass on my pancreas and that I needed a CT scan to confirm and gather more information about what the mass might be.

The following Monday I had the CT scan. My doctor called again the next day and told me the mass looked cancerous. He also said they saw an indeterminate lesion on my liver, about 1.3 x 1.3 x 1.1 cm, about the size of a large pea, that needed further investigation. Based on that, he recommended I see a gastroenterologist as the next logical step. That appointment with Arapahoe Gastroenterology was scheduled ten days later, on July 20. At that visit, the gastroenterologist told me he had ordered an endoscopic exam (EUS) to determine the nature of the pancreatic mass.

The EUS was performed at Porter Hospital in Denver on Thursday, July 23. At the end of the exam, the doctor said, "I was successful in obtaining samples from the mass on your pancreas. My initial opinion is the samples look benign, but we need to wait for the final pathology, which could take a couple of days."

One interesting detail is that I drove myself to Porter for the EUS. During check-in they told me I would not be allowed to drive home afterward. No one had told me that previously. Now what was I supposed to do?

My cancer news was still confidential, and much of the family was away. Kay was on RAGBRAI, out of state on a bike ride, and Zach was working. Daisy was home, and thankfully she had her driver's license. I had no choice. I called and asked if she could come pick me up. I told her I had a simple procedure and the hospital would not let me drive home. She picked me up, and the next morning we returned to retrieve my car from the hospital parking lot.

That same Friday afternoon, Zach, his friend Julian, and I had planned to go boating. We were just leaving the dock when I received a call from the doctor at Porter Hospital. There, while we were on the boat, he told me, "From the eight slides, we confirm that you have cancer, and it is adenocarcinoma." This is the nasty, death-sentence kind of cancer. I was in no way prepared for that news, and I was certainly not prepared to share it with anyone yet.

So… boating we went. (See reference to Appendix E, Document 1 for medical documentation.)

As it would be for anyone, receiving this diagnosis from a well-respected medical group weighed heavily on me. I was emotionally devastated, and I carried a real level of fear. For a short time longer, I had to keep the diagnosis to myself. I know that during those first two weeks I cried at times, and I cried out to God for strength and healing.

I kept the diagnosis private for two main reasons. First, Kay was away for a week on her bike ride trip, and I did not want to interrupt that time she was spending with her family, nor did I want to share such news by phone. Second, I wanted to be absolutely certain it was cancer before telling anyone. I hoped and prayed for a different diagnosis. Looking back, I now believe that keeping it to myself initially made it easier to deal with later, a strange and unexpected outcome.

With the diagnosis confirmed and so much information available online, I began researching on my own. Searches like this can provide useful and reliable information, but they can also lead you astray with partial truths. Online information is rarely specific to your exact situation, and every diagnosis is unique. I quickly realized that my cancer diagnosis was incredibly serious and that I might be dead within a year. My research only confirmed what I feared, presenting even more frightening statistics and grim life-expectancy estimates.

I knew that a normal bell-shaped curve has tails on both end, some people live longer than expected, and some live less. The left side of that curve was not encouraging. But if there was any hope, any prayer, I was determined to be on the far right side of that curve.

When you are told you have cancer, your mortality suddenly becomes very real. After moving through fear, denial, anger, and many other difficult emotions, I knew I had to focus on what my next steps should be. I was determined to continue working hard, as I always had. But I also knew I had to tell someone about my cancer, and soon.

Pancreatic Cancer Data and Facts

Pancreatic cancer is often referred to as "the king of carcinoma" due to the pancreas's hidden location deep within the body. It is the third leading cause of cancer-related deaths. It is especially deadly because it often produces few symptoms and therefore is not detected early. In many cases, the cancer has already progressed to an advanced stage by the time it is diagnosed.

The pancreas is an organ located mostly behind the stomach. It has two glandular functions: exocrine and endocrine. The exocrine function releases pancreatic juices to aid in the digestion of proteins, carbohydrates, and fats. The endocrine function releases hormones directly into the bloodstream, including insulin (which lowers blood sugar) and glucagon (which raises blood sugar), helping to maintain healthy blood sugar levels.

There are two primary kinds of pancreatic cancer:

The first arises from the exocrine cells of the pancreas and is known as adenocarcinoma. This is the type of cancer that claimed the life of actor Patrick Swayze in 2009.

The second type is called pancreatic neuroendocrine tumors (pNETs). These are named after the islands of hormone-producing cells within the pancreas. These specialized cells produce and secrete insulin, which allows cells to take in glucose from the food we eat. If this type of cancer is caught early enough, there is the potential for a longer life expectancy. This is the type of cancer that claimed the life of Steve Jobs in 2011.

pNET Subtypes and Classifications

Within pNETs (also called islet cell tumors), there are several subtypes. I will briefly summarize them here. For more detailed information, the American Cancer Society, the National Cancer Institute, and Cancer.gov are excellent resources. Where applicable, I note what applied specifically to my case.

Non-Functional (Non-Secreting) vs. Functional (Secreting):

- **Non-Functional tumors** do not produce excess hormones. They are often referred to as "silent" tumors and are usually not diagnosed until symptoms arise from their physical size, such as abdominal pain, jaundice, unexplained weight loss, or after the cancer has spread to other organs. These tumors can grow slowly. (This was my type.) These tumors are further defined by **grade and stage.**

- **Functional tumors** secrete excess hormones. The major subtypes include:

- **Insulinoma** – excess insulin (causing hypoglycemia)

- **Gastrinoma** – excess gastrin, causing Zollinger-Ellison Syndrome. Symptoms include burning stomach pain, diarrhea, nausea, vomiting, weight loss, acid reflux, and greasy stools.

- **Glucagonoma** – excess glucagon, a rare tumor leading to high blood sugar (diabetes), weight loss, diarrhea, and a painful skin rash called necrolytic migratory erythema, often affecting the mouth and tongue.

- **Somatostatinoma** – excess somatostatin, a hormone that inhibits the release of other hormones and slows digestive processes.

- **Other rare subtypes**

Grades of Pancreatic Cancer

Pancreatic tumors are also classified by grade:

- **Grade 1** – Low grade and well differentiated

- **Grade 2** – Intermediate and moderately differentiated *(This was my final diagnosis, confirmed after surgical removal of the tumor. The borders were not as clearly defined as a Grade 1.)*

- **Grade 3** – High grade and poorly differentiated. These tumors appear very abnormal and multiply faster than lower-grade tumors. *(This was how Porter Hospital classified mine based on the biopsy from the EUS.)*

Differentiation

Tumors are also described as **poorly differentiated or well differentiated.** Poorly differentiated tumors are generally more aggressive. They grow more quickly, spread more often, and carry a worse prognosis than well-differentiated tumors. The biopsy of my pancreas initially indicated that mine was poorly differentiated.

Tumor Size, Lymph Nodes, and Metastasis (TNM)

Cancer is also classified using size (T), lymph node involvement (N), and metastasis (M):

- **T (Tumor size):** The tumor sizes range from T1 to T4. *(Mine was classified as T3, meaning it was larger than T1 and T2. This was determined after surgery. When first discovered, it had been classified as T2, but it grew rapidly in the two months following surgery.)*

- **N (Lymph nodes):** These range from N0 to N3. *(I had N0, meaning no lymph node involvement at the time of surgery.)*

- **M (Metastasis):** There are types M0 and M1. *(I had M0, meaning no distant metastasis detected at that time.)*

Notable Cases: Randy Pausch and Steve Jobs

Randolph Frederick "Randy" Pausch (October 1960 – July 2008) was a professor of computer science, human-computer interaction, and design at Carnegie Mellon University in Pittsburgh, Pennsylvania. He was diagnosed with pancreatic adenocarcinoma in September 2006. In August 2007, he was given a terminal diagnosis of three to six months of good health.

Randy delivered his now-famous lecture, *"The Last Lecture: Really Achieving Your Childhood Dreams,"* in September 2007. He later co-authored a book of the same name, which became a *New York Times* bestseller. I encourage you to listen to or read it, it is excellent. Randy underwent Whipple surgery in 2006 in an effort to halt the spread of his cancer. He died from complications in July 2008.

Steve Jobs learned in 2003 that he had an extremely rare form of pancreatic cancer, an islet cell tumor (pNET). His cancer was discovered during an abdominal scan in October 2003. According to *Fortune* magazine, the scan was part of a physical exam related to ongoing gastrointestinal issues. His pNET caused high insulin levels, leading to episodes of low blood sugar, which can cause shakiness, cold sweats, nausea, vomiting, blackouts, and neurological symptoms such as impaired judgment, mood swings, irritability, apathy, and confusion.

Jobs chose to delay surgery for approximately nine months while experimenting with alternative therapies. When later scans showed the tumor had grown, he underwent surgery in July 2004. In emails to Apple employees, Jobs stated that his form of cancer "can be cured by surgical removal if diagnosed in time."

His case was more complicated than it initially appeared. He underwent a modified Whipple procedure. The extent of the surgery suggests that the cancer may have spread beyond the pancreas. It is possible that micro-metastases were already present but undetectable at the time of diagnosis, or that spread occurred during the delay while pursuing alternative treatments.

There is little debate regarding optimal treatment. "It has long been held that surgery can lead to long-term survival," says Dr. Kim. However, this surgery is no simple procedure. In some cases, only the tumor and a small amount of surrounding tissue can be removed. A

2010 analysis of cancer registries found that patients eligible for surgery, meaning the cancer had not spread beyond the pancreas, often experienced excellent outcomes, living many more years.

This is partly because neuroendocrine tumors tend to be slow-growing or indolent. Even tumors that have existed for years, and sometimes decades, often remain confined to the pancreas. In fact, this type of cancer can grow so slowly that patients sometimes die *with* it rather than *from* it. Although an estimated 2,000 to 3,000 people in the U.S. are diagnosed annually with pNETs, autopsy studies reveal many more cases in people who were never harmed by the disease.

pNET Cancer Facts

Sources: American Cancer Society, PanCAN.org, NetCancerAwareness.org, 2024

- Approximately 2% of pancreatic cancers are pNETs

- Average age at diagnosis is 60

- pNETs are rare but increasing at about 1% annually

- Occurrence rates have risen to 1.1 per 100,000 people

- It is estimated that over 300,000 people are living with pNETs

- CHAPTER 2 -

TELLING KAY MY CATACLYSMIC NEWS

After doing my research and learning about the prognosis for most people diagnosed with pancreatic cancer, I knew that Kay had to be the first to hear about my diagnosis. However, Kay was on RAGBRAI (the Register's Annual Great Bike Ride Across Iowa), a seven-day bike ride that runs from Sunday to Saturday. She attended the event with friends and family and normally would arrive home on Sunday night. This news was not something I wanted to share over the phone.

God was in control, and I received an incredible blessing. Kay called to tell me they were cutting that year's bike ride short, a first. Wow. I knew God was in the details. This change meant she would be home sooner, which allowed me to share my unwelcome news face to face. She would be home on Friday evening, and Daisy had a Westernaires event the next day. My decision was made. I would tell Kay my news during the break between events.

Keeping this life-changing diagnosis to myself had become very difficult. I needed to share it with Kay so she could help me navigate this new and distressing reality of life with cancer.

I prayed to God and trusted Him for strength and support. It was still very early in my journey. I had not yet thought deeply about my future or how much my life might change as a result of this diagnosis. I do remember thinking, sometime in my early fifties, that I might someday get cancer like my father and die before reaching the age of fifty-nine, the age at which Dad died. At the time, it was more of a passing thought. Now it was real. I was fifty-seven. My intermittent fear had come true, and I was even younger than Dad. Thankfully, those thoughts never fully consumed me.

I had read that telling others you have cancer, especially those you love most, is one of the hardest things you will ever do. I absolutely agree with that statement. There is never an appropriate time to share news like this. At that point, our marriage was not in a particularly good place, which made telling Kay even harder. I did not know how she would respond. Would she become distant or emotionally removed because she did not want to deal with it, or with me? Or would she stand beside me throughout the journey?

At the beginning of a break during the Westernaires event, I told Kay that I needed to talk with her and asked if we could go outside. I had not rehearsed. I had no idea how I was going to say it or what words I would use. I simply blurted it out, through tears and overwhelming emotion, that I had been diagnosed with pancreatic cancer.

Disbelief is one of the first reactions when you are told you have cancer. That was true for me, and it was true for Kay as well. As the news began to sink in, we talked through what this might mean and what our options were. We could not have imagined this happening to us.

I was incredibly blessed to have Kay by my side. She became my strongest supporter, and she was amazing. Her response was thoughtful, loving, and exactly what I needed. From the moment I told her about my diagnosis, we became a team. We shared a common goal, to face this challenge head-on and do everything possible to overcome it. We talked through what each of us would do next, and from that day forward we grew together in many ways. Our faith in God deepened, our trust in Him to carry us through this ordeal strengthened, and our commitment to one another in marriage grew stronger as well.

As I mentioned earlier, some people find their faith shaken by cancer. Ours was not. I cannot fully explain why or how that was possible. I only know that God was holding our hands.

How did cancer change my outlook on life and my long-term goals? I was convinced that my time on earth would be shortened. I do not remember ever feeling hopeless, though I certainly felt disheartened at times. My research suggested I had eight to twelve months to live. When we shared the news with our children, I promised them that I would be there for their life milestones. Did I truly believe that promise? Looking back, I think I did, though perhaps not with the confidence I might have had under different circumstances.

Still, I believe that maintaining a positive attitude and continuing my pre-cancer activities, within reason, was an important goal. Did I think about life differently after my diagnosis? Absolutely. I had moments of fear and deep uncertainty. But I refused to allow those thoughts to overtake my determination to remain positive.

As I shared my diagnosis with more people, I noticed changes in how some of them treated me. When people said things like, "You look good," "Everything will be okay," or "I have a good feeling about this," I assumed they simply did not know what to say, or they did not want me to feel discouraged. How could they know what to say if they had never been diagnosed with cancer themselves?

Generally, I chose to ignore remarks like these. I was not hurt by them, but I was disappointed. I took such comments to mean they did not want to have a real conversation about my cancer, likely because it made them uncomfortable. This became even more noticeable later, when people knew I had started chemotherapy.

Chemotherapy can dramatically affect how a person looks and feels. Many expect you to appear weak, lose your hair, or look fragile. Looking back, I do not recall anyone who stopped being my friend. Most of my friends, often identifiable by the tone of their voice or the way they looked at me, expressed genuine concern and offered meaningful help. Before my own diagnosis, I believe I would have reacted in much the same way if a friend had been facing a similar illness.

CHAPTER 3

UNDERSTANDING AND SHARING MY NEWS

University Hospital Visit

Kay and I agreed that I would contact Dr. Carroll, a well-known invasive cardiologist at University Hospital (UH) in Denver, who was also a former client of mine. He was immediately helpful and made several phone calls on my behalf. He spoke with the chairman of surgery, who recommended two surgeons with the most experience performing the complicated Whipple operation in our local area. This surgery involves removal of the head of the pancreas, gallbladder, bile duct, the first part of the small intestine and reconnecting the remaining organs. Dr. Carroll assured us that he would help to "grease the skids" if needed. He also emphasized to me that the highest priority was to get highly competent consultations as soon as possible so you can decide where and with whom to proceed with treatment. Through his assistance, we were able to secure a prompt appointment with one of the recommended surgeons.

Within a couple of days, in late July, Kay and I found ourselves at UH for the first of what would become many visits with medical professionals. We met with a surgical oncologist and his assistant and were impressed by their professionalism and thoroughness. They ordered additional blood work and other tests and, based on those results, indicated that my surgery needed to be done very soon. The surgical oncologist shared that he performed approximately twelve Whipple surgeries each year. He also explained that the risk of postoperative complications was quite high—over forty percent.

His surgical schedule, however, was booked out for nearly three months. He also explained that he performed the Whipple using the "open" approach, sometimes called the "bucket-handle" approach. With this method, the surgeon makes a U-shaped incision around the abdomen, allowing full access to the pancreas and surrounding organs. This approach can make it easier to remove the affected organs and reattach the small intestine. The next day, we also met with a university radiologist, who conducted additional imaging tests.

A few days later, the surgeon called us late in the evening with unexpected news. Based on their test results and additional information, he said he was reasonably confident that I did not have adenocarcinoma. Instead, he believed I had the rarer form of pancreatic cancer previously mentioned, a pancreatic neuroendocrine tumor (pNET). He ordered one additional blood test, Chromogranin A (CgA), which is a tumor marker for pNETs, also referred to as carcinoid cancers. This phone call was an "up" on our roller coaster ride, even though we did not yet fully understand what this new diagnosis meant.

(See appendix E, Document 2 for medical documentation.)

Now we had a different diagnosis, and once again we needed to do more research. From what we learned, pNETs are generally slower-growing cancers. This also suggested that I might have had cancer for at least a year, and possibly several years. In a very short period of time, I had received two dramatically different diagnoses. Because of this experience, I strongly encourage anyone facing a serious medical condition to seek a second opinion, and perhaps even a third or fourth. Ultimately, that is exactly what I did.

Was this new diagnosis a sign of hope? Could it even be a miracle? This new diagnosis came only days after our meeting with this surgeon and just ten days after the original pathology report confirmed adenocarcinoma. A pNET is a rarer and less aggressive cancer, a "better" cancer, if there is such a thing. Skeptics might suggest that the original diagnosis was wrong, or that the University made an error. I believe both diagnoses were accurate at the times they were made. I find it difficult to believe that the endoscopic ultrasound procedure, which removed actual tissue samples from my pancreas, would have retrieved incorrect tissue, or that a pathologist would misread eight separate slides. It had to be God. How else could one explain such a dramatic change in diagnosis? Even if you do not believe in God, it is hard not to see this as miraculous.

I was elated by this new and more hopeful diagnosis. I felt as though I was on a new journey, one unlike anything I had ever experienced before. I believed I had no choice but to follow wherever this path led Kay and me. At that point, I trusted every doctor and accepted their words at face value. As my journey continued, however, my confidence in diagnoses and recommendations began to shift, and I found myself asking more questions and seeking greater clarity.

We hoped this surgeon could perform my Whipple surgery, but his schedule was already booked for months. Kay and I continued exploring other options. Kay contacted MD Anderson and the Cancer Centers of America. I made similar calls, including one to the Mayo Clinic in Rochester, Minnesota, which was ranked among the top three cancer centers in the country according to *U.S. News & World Report.* I checked with my insurance carrier and learned that Mayo Clinic was in-network, another incredible blessing. We researched hospitals as far away as New York, comparing statistics related to the Whipple procedure. To build trust and confidence, we wanted both a facility and a surgeon with extensive experience performing this complex surgery. By the end of July, we had completed our research.

Sharing Our News with Family

It was now time to share our news with our children and others. We had no idea how or what to say. On a Thursday afternoon, we met with Pastor Bruce from The Rock of the Southwest Church, where we had been attending for a couple of years. We asked for his advice on how best to share this news with our children. I was in tears through much of that conversation. It was incredibly difficult to talk about my diagnosis without becoming emotional.

Based on how teary-eyed I was, Pastor Bruce said it would be even harder for us to tell our children. He offered helpful guidance, suggesting that we state the facts clearly and quickly so Zach and Daisy could begin to process and absorb the news.

That evening, we told our children that we needed to meet with them to share something important. After telling them that I had cancer, I promised Daisy that I would be there for her high school graduation and other milestones. I also promised Zach that I would be there for his college graduation; he was nearing his nineteenth birthday. It was an incredibly difficult conversation for all of us. We shared our next steps, but I honestly do not remember how the meeting ended. Do you stand up and leave? Do you hug? I simply do not recall. Telling our children was one of the hardest things I have ever done. It was an emotional tempest, but Kay and I navigated it together.

Sharing the news with other family members and friends was somewhat easier, as those conversations could take place over the phone. Still, nothing compared to telling our children.

After that, Kay and I began contacting the rest of our family. I called Brian, who was living in Europe at the time with his wife Heather and their family. I also called Don and Bill, as well as each of my sisters, to share my diagnosis and our planned next steps. We promised to keep them informed as my cancer journey began in earnest.

My sister Mary had not spoken with me or my siblings for many years, and I was unsure whether I would even be able to reach her. I remember calling her from work, and to my surprise, she answered. I told her that I had been diagnosed with pancreatic cancer and then paused. I heard her gasp. She allowed me to speak a bit longer about what lay ahead before ending the call. I was grateful for the opportunity to share my news with her. God is so good.

- CHAPTER 4 -
MAYO, THOUGHTS AND MY LIFE VERSE

Mayo Clinic Initial Visit with Mixed Reviews

My diagnosis was serious, and I was facing a complicated surgery. One personal goal I had always carried was to outlive my parents, and now I was unsure by how much. Life continued for all of us, and as friends and people from church learned of my diagnosis, prayers on my behalf began to pour in.

We decided that our first visit should be to the Mayo Clinic in Rochester, Minnesota. I contacted Mayo and asked for help arranging appointments with the appropriate specialists. They requested copies of all my imaging, blood work, and physician notes. I gathered everything and sent it via FedEx. During this time, I had several phone conversations with the assistant to the head of the gastroenterology department, with whom we were scheduled to meet.

Mayo Clinic scheduled several appointments for our initial visit: blood tests, a CT scan, a meeting with a gastroenterologist, a consultation with a pancreatic surgeon, and a biopsy of the spot on my liver. We booked our flights, rented a car, and traveled to Rochester for three days in mid-August 2009. Before leaving, I knew I had to inform my boss, George Pardos, of my diagnosis and discuss how we might manage my work responsibilities. I asked him to keep the information confidential, which he graciously did.

Mayo completed their testing in the morning, and we met first with a resident who worked under the head of the gastroenterology department. He was pleasant and professional. After speaking with us, he said he would notify the doctor that we were ready to see him. Shortly afterward, the doctor entered the room. Kay and I began asking questions about the prior tests we had sent and the results from the tests Mayo had run that morning.

His response stunned us. He said, "Why would I look at your chart ahead of time? If I did that, I would never get anything done, and since you only have eight months to live, it would be a waste of my time." Kay and I were shocked. We silently wondered why we had gone to the effort of sending all my medical records. He ignored our questions, especially Kay's, and made us feel as if she was not even in the room, as though she was not worth addressing.

We had come to the highly esteemed Mayo Clinic believing we would encounter the best physicians in the world. When the brief interaction ended, the doctor left the room and his assistant returned. We shared how deeply displeased and shaken we were by the doctor's attitude and words. We asked how we could formally communicate our experience to Mayo. He told us we would receive a survey. We never did.

We left that appointment shocked and disappointed. Once again, we felt ourselves spiraling downward. Porter Hospital's pathology report said adenocarcinoma. The University Hospital doctor told us it was a pNET. Now, a Mayo Clinic physician was agreeing with the original adenocarcinoma diagnosis and giving me eight months to live. I believe his conclusion was based on a very limited review of my medical records and that he had not considered the University Hospital findings at all.

The Mayo ultrasound showed the same mass on the right lobe of my liver that had appeared on the earlier CT scan. Mayo proceeded with the planned biopsy the following day. When the procedure was finished, the doctor said the liver sample did not appear cancerous, though the lab would confirm it. I was so overwhelmed with relief that I welled up with tears.

Later that same day, we met with Dr. Thompson, a pancreatic surgeon at Mayo Clinic. He was genuinely kind and immediately restored our hope. He shared a story about a patient with a diagnosis similar to mine on whom he had performed a Whipple surgery fifteen years earlier. That patient was now living in Colorado, skiing, and thriving.

Dr. Thompson explained that he was no longer performing Whipple surgeries on a regular basis, but despite being booked out two or more months, he offered to perform mine if needed. He recommended that we also meet with Dr. Kendrick and another pancreatic surgeon who were now performing most of Mayo's Whipple procedures. He said he would tentatively schedule my surgery and that we could cancel if we chose one of his colleagues. Once again, our emotional roller coaster climbed upward.

Later that day, we received the official liver biopsy results. The lesion was identified as a cavernous hemangioma—benign. This meant my cancer had not spread. We were deeply encouraged. Pancreatic cancer often metastasizes to the liver and sometimes to the lungs, so this result allowed us to focus on one major decision: where and with whom should I undergo my Whipple surgery?

My Frame of Mind About My Cancer

I knew cancer would bring substantial changes to my life, but I had no idea how far-reaching those changes would be. Even now, I do not fully understand all the ways it has affected me and my family. At the time, I simply wanted to continue doing what was necessary and expected of me, especially continuing to work so I could provide for my family. I also wanted to enjoy life to whatever extent that might still be possible.

I continued going to work each day, which was a blessing because it helped keep my mind off my cancer. I did not know whether I could beat it. Each day brought new realizations about how I felt and what I wanted. At times, it was difficult to maintain the same level of focus I had before my diagnosis. Colleagues wanted to show their support and often shared stories about their own families or friends who had faced serious illnesses.

For anyone who has received a troubling diagnosis, the power of a positive outlook cannot be overstated, though it often requires tremendous effort. I discovered that with a positive outlook, I became more alert, more alive, and more appreciative of each day. It truly becomes a second chance to do good, to be more compassionate and loving, and to surrender your struggles to the Lord. When you hear words like "stable," "in remission," or "cancer-free," you begin to breathe easier and life slowly returns to something close to normal.

You can live life the same as before diagnosis, or you can live an enhanced life, one in which every day is recognized as a true blessing from God. You live content and grateful for however much time you have been given.

Many cancers, especially pancreatic cancer, feel like death sentences; it becomes a question of when, not if. For some, that time is measured in weeks; for others, it may be years. It can be an isolating experience. People often do not know what to say or how to act. When encountering someone facing cancer, serious illness, or profound loss, I suggest honesty. Phrases like, "I don't know what to say" and "I can't imagine what you're going through" felt genuine to me. Sometimes, a hug was offered and appreciated. Having walked this road, I now understand better how much simply being there matters.

During this period, I felt compelled to write detailed end-of-life wishes. I wrote letters to Kay, my children, and my sisters. I truly did not expect to live very long. Those letters, which I have updated once or twice, remain in our home safe for whenever my time does come.

After our Mayo visit, coworkers often asked how I could remain so positive. My response was always the same: "Why would I be any other way?" I knew a negative attitude would only worsen my outcome. Cancer became my new normal. I had nothing to be angry about, and the fact that I was asymptomatic made it easier to remain upbeat. Still, the statistics reminded me that difficult days were ahead.

Our priorities shifted instantly. New goals emerged. Time for doctor visits, surgery, chemotherapy, and recovery had to be carved out of already full lives. Yet somehow, we made room by letting go of what mattered less. Maintaining a positive attitude became a habit, one that helped sustain me.

As we became more involved with a church we were attending in Fairplay, friends there offered constant encouragement. Jim, a retired pastor, often told me, "God is not done with you." Those words resonated deeply. I now pass them on whenever I sense someone needs to hear them.

Back at work, the words spoken by the Mayo doctor continued to sting. I shared that experience with George, who encouraged us not to judge the entire institution based on one physician. Other doctor friends echoed his advice. Taking their counsel to heart, Kay and I gathered our courage and returned to Mayo Clinic for surgery.

My Whipple surgery was scheduled for September 15, 2009, sooner than the university hospital could schedule it and with surgeons who had far more experience. We prepared for what we expected would be a two-to-three-week stay. I reviewed bell-curve data showing the average Whipple hospitalization was about two weeks. I was certain I would beat that average. I did, but on the wrong side of the curve. Still, it felt good to have our decisions made. We believed we had done our homework. We were heading back to Mayo Clinic for surgery.

My Life Verse

On August 30, 2009, just weeks after my diagnosis, I watched a sermon at our cabin. The message was based on Isaiah 41:10. Pastor Daniel spoke about faith and courage, drawing from Scripture and writers like C.S. Lewis. That sermon changed my life. Isaiah 41:10 became my Life Verse:

> *"So do not fear, for I am with you;*
> *do not be dismayed, for I am your God.*
> *I will strengthen you and help you;*
> *I will uphold you with my righteous right hand."*

"Do not be afraid" is one of the most repeated phrases in the Bible, underscoring its importance in God's message to us. This verse came just two weeks before my surgery, exactly when I would need it most. I still pray it regularly, especially before major tests or procedures, and I return to it again and again.

- CHAPTER 5 -

MAYO, SURGERY, AND HOSPITALIZATION

Going Back to Mayo

The most common way to gain access to Mayo Clinic is through a referral, usually from your primary care physician or surgeon. This often occurs because your doctor believes your case is unique, unusually complex, or better suited to the specialized care Mayo provides. A word of caution: your doctor or surgeon may not want to lose your treatment or surgical revenue by referring you to another care center. It is also possible that your insurance plan, especially HMOs or closed systems like Kaiser, does not allow easy access to Mayo. With an open-panel plan, such as a PPO or traditional insurance plan, you generally have more choices. It is always worth checking with your insurance carrier to fully understand your options. I was fortunate that my employer's group health insurance allowed access to multiple centers of excellence.

I believe my self-referral to a specialized care center was somewhat rare in 2009. Many friends and family members asked who referred me to Mayo, and even Mayo staff frequently asked me who my referring physician was. I always explained that I did not have one. I was confident my primary care doctor would have gladly provided a referral had I asked, since he readily admitted he had little experience with pancreatic cancer and was supportive of my choice to pursue care at Mayo. The disadvantage of self-referral, however, is that you must do all the legwork yourself, gathering medical records, imaging, test results, medical history, and ensuring everything arrives at Mayo well in advance of your visit.

Because I sought out Mayo Clinic on my own, we were responsible for making all appointments and covering our travel, lodging, meals, and other out-of-pocket expenses. This was only possible because I had followed God's leading in selling my businesses earlier, which placed our family in a financial position to afford this care. I am so very grateful that I listened and followed His direction. Some employers offer supplemental insurance that can help cover travel and lodging expenses related to specialized medical care. I would strongly recommend such coverage to anyone who can afford it (for example, Aflac). If you wait until after a diagnosis of cancer, heart disease, or another serious illness, it will be too late; your application will almost certainly be denied.

Mayo Clinic and its hospitals in Rochester, Minnesota, are exceptional facilities. Their campus includes downtown Rochester and Saint Mary's Hospital, located about ten blocks west of downtown. Mayo Clinic Hospital has over 2,000 beds and thirty-seven operating rooms, while Saint Mary's has approximately 1,300 beds and seventy operating rooms. In 2009, Mayo operated two hospitals in a city of just over 100,000 people, employed roughly 3,700 physicians, and more than 56,000 additional staff and residents. They see over one million patients annually and are consistently ranked among the nation's top three hospitals across numerous specialties.

One aspect of Mayo's system that stood out to me was their scheduling philosophy. They make every effort to schedule diagnostic tests in the morning so that patients can meet with physicians later the same day to review results. In many other healthcare systems at that time, tests were performed on one day, results sent to outside labs, and follow-up appointments scheduled days later, often delaying diagnosis and treatment decisions. Mayo's approach significantly reduced the time patients spent waiting and worrying.

Since 2009, this process has improved at many medical centers, but at the time, Mayo's system was far ahead of most. Their approach often allows patients to return home after just one or two nights, already knowing their results and treatment recommendations. Some cases do take longer, especially if extensive testing or consultations with multiple specialists are required. At Mayo, physicians collaborate closely, often discussing cases together to determine the best course of action, sometimes even before or after your visit without the patient present.

Despite the serious and often unwelcome news delivered there, I found the Mayo Clinic campus to be peaceful and calming. Many buildings are connected by enclosed walkways, allowing patients to move throughout the campus protected from the weather. Volunteers provide comfort through live music, playing piano and singing throughout the day. God's presence and love felt evident to me while we were there. You sense that compassionate, high-quality care is the priority; this is so important since nearly everyone coming to Mayo faces a difficult diagnosis.

The Whipple Surgery

We arrived in Rochester, Minnesota, on Sunday, September 13, 2009, with my Whipple surgery scheduled for Tuesday. On Monday, I underwent a CT scan and additional blood work. We also had two appointments scheduled with pancreatic surgeons recommended by Dr. Thompson during our previous visit. When we arrived, we were quickly informed that Dr. Kendrick was fully booked and would not be able to meet with us. His surgery schedule was also filled for the next three weeks.

I had reservations about the "bucket" or open surgical approach, which both the University Hospital surgeon and the other Mayo surgeon used. Our research over the previous month convinced me that I preferred a laparoscopic Whipple if possible. This method uses five small incisions rather than a large abdominal incision, and recovery is often easier. Dr. Kendrick was the only surgeon at Mayo performing the Whipple laparoscopically.

Since Dr. Kendrick was unavailable, we were offered the option to return in three weeks to meet with him and schedule surgery. This was not acceptable. We had already coordinated extended absences with my employer, arranged care for Daisy, and incurred significant travel costs. Delaying surgery also felt medically unwise. To say we were disappointed would be an understatement.

We met with the surgeon who performed the open approach and were impressed by his professionalism and competence. We signed consent forms allowing him to perform my surgery the next morning. Immediately after signing, a nurse entered the room and told us that Dr. Kendrick had unexpectedly become available and could meet with us after all. In fact, he was on his way.

Dr. Kendrick arrived shortly thereafter and spoke with us kindly and confidently. After reviewing my chart, he was certain I had a pNET. He also told us he could perform my surgery the next day. He explained that he would begin laparoscopically and convert to an open procedure only if necessary. That sounded ideal. We tore up the previous consent forms and signed new ones with Dr. Kendrick.

We were truly blessed. God was clearly in the details, holding our hands. Minutes earlier, surgery with our preferred physician seemed impossible; now it was happening. Dr. Kendrick spent a generous amount of time with us and proudly noted that I would be his sixty-third laparoscopic Whipple patient. I was scheduled for surgery the very next day.

I slept reasonably well the night before surgery, despite the gravity of what lay ahead. I was told to arrive at the hospital by 9:00 a.m. for a 1:00 p.m. surgery. A Whipple procedure is a major operation, typically lasting anywhere from six to ten hours. That morning, news broke that actor Patrick Swayze had died following his battle with pancreatic cancer. If I needed further confirmation of how serious my diagnosis was, that was it, on the very day of my surgery.

Late that morning, I was taken to the pre-operative area. I kissed Kay and said, "Goodbye, I'll see you later." Kay remained in the waiting room, with our future sister-in-law staying with her part of the day. It was an incredibly long day for her, nearly twelve hours of waiting, praying, worrying, and hoping.

My life often followed a pattern of hurry up and wait, and this day was no exception. I was prepped, vitals were taken, IVs were started, and then I waited, lying on the pre-op table in a large room divided by curtains. I overheard other patients describing their conditions to nurses and residents. Many sounded far worse off than me.

I remembered the saying, "There is always someone worse off than you," and it rang true.

God was with me. I felt completely at peace, something that surprised me. This peace was unlike anything I had felt before. Previously, before procedures such as lithotripsy, hernia repair, or eye surgery, I remembered being cold and shivering. Not today. I had a profound feeling of great peace. God was not only holding my hand, but he was taking my hand and lifting it up, and He was bringing me up with it, as I realized God's got this, and I immediately felt amazing comfort. I prayed my life verse repeatedly, Isaiah 41:10. I truly felt that God had this under control.

How was I able to be so at peace before such a major surgery? I believe it came from fully trusting God. It never crossed my mind that I might not survive, even though that was a real possibility. I recalled the promise I had made to my children weeks earlier, that I would be there for them. I accepted my situation and moved forward, trusting God completely.

> *"Blessed is the one who perseveres under trial because, having stood the test, that person will receive the crown of life that the Lord has promised to those who love him."* (James 1:12)

Finally, it was time. I was wheeled into the operating room, saw the nurses, staff, and Dr. Kendrick near my head. He asked me a question or two, and then I drifted into a deep sleep.

Kay kept a large network of friends and family updated throughout my surgery and recovery, emailing and calling so they could pray. I had no idea how extensive this prayer network was until much later. God heard every one of those prayers.

St. Mary's – The Long Hospital Stay

I was formally admitted to Saint Mary's Hospital late that evening. My first brief memory was seeing Kay standing beside me as nurses transferred me onto my bed. It was around eleven p.m. I drifted back to sleep and did not fully awaken until the next morning, when I learned more about what had happened during surgery.

Dr. Kendrick visited that morning and explained that the surgery had gone well, but it had taken longer and was more complicated than expected. The tumor was larger than anticipated and had wrapped around my superior mesenteric vein. This vein is a major blood vessel supplying the liver, spleen, and stomach, making it critical and difficult to work around. The tumor they removed was about the size of a golf ball, much larger than the grape-sized mass seen in July. This growth made laparoscopic removal extremely challenging.

The tumor was classified as T3, larger than four centimeters, but still confined to the pancreas. (See Appendix E, Document 3 for medical document)

On September 18th, the surgical pathology results arrived and confirmed that my cancer was the rarer form. This was further proof of my miracle. My diagnosis had been changed from adenocarcinoma to a pNET, as mentioned earlier, by God during that original ten-day period—from the Porter EUS pathology to the time we met with the doctor at University Hospital.

As Dr. Kendrick continued, he told us that I had been his second Whipple surgery the day before. We were shocked. How could he mentally and physically perform two surgeries back-to-back, each lasting six to ten hours? When we asked him, he simply responded, "I do it all the time."

The care provided by the hospital staff was incredible. Because of my lengthy stay, I came to know the nurses well, most of whom worked twelve-hour shifts. This allowed for excellent continuity of care. Dr. Kendrick visited every day. Since Mayo is a teaching hospital, three to four residents always accompanied him. These residents had between one and three years of training and visited more frequently, sometimes two or more times per day, depending on my condition and recovery status. Blood was typically drawn early each morning, often around six o'clock, placed in a canister, and sent through a vacuum tube to the downtown clinic. By the time Dr. Kendrick made his morning rounds, the results were available so he could review and discuss them with us.

It is strange what the mind recalls vividly versus what it does not recall at all. Much of the first two weeks was a blur, and I remember very little besides the pain I was in. During those first two weeks, I became less optimistic about my future. I questioned some of my decisions: Why did I have this surgery? Was this pain worth it?

I experienced three major types of pain. The first was from the gas in my abdomen as a result of choosing laparoscopic surgery over the open approach. The second was related to not having a bowel movement. The third was due to infection. There was also, of course, pain from the surgery itself. I almost always had the option to give myself morphine by pulling a small trigger, but this caused significant nausea. As a result, I tried to avoid using morphine whenever possible. In addition to these pains, I also developed a severe case of hiccups, an additional annoyance on top of everything else. The hiccups lasted for five days.

I found that nurses were often better than doctors at comforting and caring for patients. They spend far more time with patients than doctors do, especially in the ICU. I like to joke and kid around,

I often use wordplay, so I tried to bring that same approach to my interactions with nurses and doctors. In most cases, it helped ease the atmosphere and warm those interactions. When I think back on the nearly four weeks I spent in the hospital, it is difficult to imagine. I am normally active and constantly on the move, always doing something.

Up to this point, no one had clearly stated what stage my cancer was or used specific descriptive terms. I assumed it might not matter much with pancreatic cancer because of its low survival rate. I eventually learned that many terms are used to describe pNET cancers. What I learned was that mine was Stage I, non-secreting, and, after God changed my diagnosis, it was moderately differentiated. I do not understand most medical terminology, though I explained some of it earlier in the book.

Like most things, laparoscopic surgery has both advantages and disadvantages. I was so certain that I did not want open surgery that I did not fully explore the potential downsides. One major drawback of the laparoscopic approach is the gas introduced into the abdominal cavity to create working space. This gas can remain after surgery and cause bloating, cramps, and even shoulder pain due to irritation of the diaphragm. I experienced severe bloating and cramping, which led me to second-guess my decision. I later learned that open surgery would have provided easier access for tumor removal and intestinal reattachment. I also believe my infection may have been related to the laparoscopic approach. Still, the thought of a large U-shaped incision across my abdomen was difficult to accept, and the choice was ultimately mine.

My post-surgery recovery became the familiar roller coaster, setbacks and complications mixed with encouraging news. The following candid letter, which I wrote to my sister Barbara from my hospital bed, reflects how I viewed my situation at the time:

Wednesday wasn't too bad. Thursday through Sunday went down-hill with a lot of pain. Monday through today has been steadily improving, and the pain is mostly manageable. I hope to start eating something other than Liquid IVs again in a day or two. Some body systems still need to start working again, mainly my bowels.

This surgery has a predicted complication rate of about 40 percent, and I didn't beat the odds this time. I experienced internal bleeding and leaking at the surgical site.

The great news is that on Friday we met with medical oncology, and they indicated that I am cancer-free, no cancer in the lymph nodes. The cancer had not spread, and they removed enough healthy tissue to ensure all the bad cells were gone. If it ever returns, since it is slow-growing, I may never need to do much about it. I will, however, have regular checkups.

Because of the complications, I will likely be at Mayo for about one more week, but there is no better place to be. They perform this surgery often and have extensive recovery experience. The nurses are highly specialized and wonderful to work with, and the doctors stop by twice a day.

We chose Mayo Clinic for reasons beyond reputation; it was closer to family and friends than other options we considered. This allowed Kay access to transportation and a place to rest during the early part of my recovery. One particularly difficult moment for Kay was celebrating her birthday while I was still hospitalized. I cannot imagine how disappointing it must have been for her to spend her birthday in a hospital room while I recovered.

You might wonder whether my faith was shaken or tested. Absolutely, it has been tested many times throughout my life, but never enough to make my faith disappear. As you have read, both Kay and I experienced many ups and downs, much like a roller coaster.

- CHAPTER 6 -

THE VISITATION, POST-RECOVERY, AND HOME

The Miracle: Jesus' Visitation

Ten days after surgery, I was not improving as I had hoped. I would make small gains here and there, then relapse and grow worse again. This cycle was taking a toll on my mental health and on my hope for the future. But then something happened that strengthened my faith—one day that stands out above all the rest, by a mile. It was day eleven, Saturday, September 26th, 2009.

I could not sleep that night because of intense pain. I turned my head to look at the clock on my right, and saw it was one in the morning. Then I turned my head to the left, and there I beheld something unbelievable. By my left shoulder I saw Jesus—and a woman with Him. Jesus was a wonderful and welcome sight; I knew Him.

He spoke these words to me: "My beloved Son, with whom I am well pleased" (Jesus loves to quote Scripture—words from Matthew 3:17). Then He continued, "Today you will have a very rough day, but you will get better." Jesus and the woman departed from my sight as quickly as they had come.

At the time, I did not know for sure who the woman was. Several months later I realized it was Mother Mary. I was in St. Mary's Hospital, and that is exactly how God would orchestrate it. There was no doubt who Jesus was, though. He was as one might imagine Him to be.

What did He look and sound like? I wish I could describe Jesus in intimate detail. Both Jesus and Mary were clothed in the historical Hebrew garments of His earthly life. His voice was heard only by me; I do not believe it would have been audible to anyone else. He had a beard and moderately long hair. His appearance was the same as the time He visited me during my divorce, though then His whole body was present. This time, both He and Mother Mary were visible from the shoulders upward. She wore a sheitel, the traditional Hebrew head covering, and only her face was visible.

I had to reach into the recesses of my mind for other details, and I remember thinking Jesus had blue eyes, which I later told Kay. However, most of my research indicated He would probably have brown eyes, since that was the prevailing eye color in the Middle East at that time. I remembered a book I had read, *Heaven Is for Real* by Todd Burpo, in which his son described Jesus in detail. I also read an account of a woman named Carol Meyer who had a near death experience in the 1960's who also had a vision of Jesus describing Him in much the same way as Todd Burpo's son described him. Both their descriptions matched each other closely and also matched an image Akiane Kramarik drew called *Prince of Peace*. She was four years old when she said she saw Jesus. The drawing shows Jesus with blue eyes, confirmation of what I recalled.

However, all those physical details were not what mattered. What mattered was the power of His presence and His words. His visit comforted me, reassured me that I had made the right choice, and helped me make decisions that kept me focused on continuing to fight, despite my exhaustion and pain. I had no idea what lay ahead. To this day, His visit dramatically changed the level of my faith and trust in Him.

Kay was staying at a friend of the family's house that night. I wanted so badly to tell her about the incredible visit from Jesus. But when Kay arrived at the hospital early the next morning, I was unable to talk. My pain had increased to excruciating levels, and nurses were constantly in the room. By that afternoon I was vomiting blood, and I experienced syncopal episodes, I became unconscious and limp, then shortly recovered. Kay saw it happen. She later told me she ran into the hospital corridor and yelled for help, thinking I had died. I was Code Blue for about thirty seconds and then I came to. I had lost a lot of blood, and my white blood cell count had gone through the roof almost double the normal range; 21,000 (see Appendix E, Document 4 for medical documentation).

I passed out again. When I came to, doctors and nurses were looking down at me, saying, "Dan, Dan, can you hear me?" I was unnerved and frightened that it might happen again. They made the decision to move me to the intensive care unit (ICU). I remained there for three days. Prior to that day, I had already been given seven units of blood. On that first day in the ICU, I was given four more units. (One unit of blood is roughly the equivalent of one pint.)

My rising white blood cell count indicated an infection, and I was told they might need to perform another surgery to clean out the excess blood that had accumulated. The drain tube was not working as they expected. They performed another CT scan and still could not locate where the internal bleeding was coming from. I knew I did not want another surgery, no matter the reason.

August 2022: A Confirmation in My Chart

In August 2022, while researching and preparing for my first formal presentation of my cancer and healing story, which I call "My Testimony", I came upon something astounding. I was presenting at Redemption Hills Church to a men's group of about thirty, composed of family, friends, and church members (some believers and some not). I thought it would be fascinating to see what the doctor had written in my medical record on September 26.

I logged into Mayo's patient portal and pulled up the doctor's notes. I was blown away. The doctor had written, with a date stamp of 9:38 p.m. that day: "Mr. Zebarth is having a rough day." The exact words Jesus spoke to me at one in the morning.

God is so awesome! I found it deeply reassuring that Jesus' words to me were the exact same words the doctor later wrote in my chart. Those are unusual words for a doctor to use when there are so many medical phrases available, such as "patient in distress" or "acutely unwell," and the like. To me, it proved how real Jesus' visit was and that His words were repeated by the doctor and preserved in my chart as independent confirmation more than twenty hours later.

The miracle of Jesus' visit made the rest of my recovery tolerable. Without His visit, I would not have had the strength, commitment, or motivation to continue my fight against cancer. Before that day, I had second thoughts about my decision to go through with the surgery and everything this ordeal was becoming. I believe I would have given up. The abdominal pain was so intense. If you have ever experienced strong or persistent pain, you will understand how easily it can cloud your thinking. In that state, it becomes difficult to think rationally or objectively. A positive attitude is hard to maintain, and that, I believe, is when doubt enters your mind. The enemy (the devil) thrives when you are in this condition, and it becomes difficult to find peace or rest. Many people fail to realize that the primary battle in our lives takes place in the spiritual realm, which can then influence our physical thoughts and emotions.

Jesus' visit changed my life and my outlook from that day forward. A visit from Jesus is not something you forget. It helped me press doubt out of my mind more easily. I became hopeful again, and my attitude changed with that renewed hope. From that experience, I felt empowered to tell others about His visit without worrying whether they would believe me or not. It truly does not matter whether they believe it. I was there, and I have firsthand knowledge of that experience. Interestingly, when I share my story, some people tell me they have experienced something similar, or they know someone who has. I have also become more interested in faith-based, real-life stories and documentaries. I find comfort in them, and they help reinforce my faith. I often find myself comparing notes with the stories I read, watch, or hear.

That day, I nearly died. Yet I am alive today because of Jesus' words and His visit that morning. It has forever changed me in so many ways. I did get better in the days that followed, just as Jesus said. He does not lie. God is so good, and He held my hand.

Throughout this cancer challenge, my marriage with Kay was also being healed and strengthened. From day eleven onward, Kay rarely left my side. I cannot say that everything in our marriage became perfect, and even today we still have challenges. I continue to have other medical issues, and I know I will face more in the future. But it is all worthwhile, knowing that Jesus loves and cares for me—and for you. I know that my place in Heaven is secure, and it will be glorious when I eventually go to my heavenly home.

Post-Surgery Recovery at St. Mary's

Despite my visit from Jesus, my recovery still included many difficult days. Doctors and nurses encouraged me to walk frequently up and down the hospital hallways. Walking was painful, and to be honest, it was also very boring. A few times, when the weather allowed, we went outside to the courtyard, which was much more pleasant. I knew walking would help speed my recovery, but forcing myself to do it was challenging. Looking back, I wish I had pushed myself harder to walk more often.

After my extraordinary visit from Jesus, I gradually improved. From that point on, my recovery became more consistent. I was seen daily by residents, nurses, and other specialists, and Dr. Kendrick visited almost every day. I had frequent blood work—nearly every day—as well as ECGs, CT scans, and other tests. As mentioned earlier, I experienced post-operative gastrointestinal bleeding, a leak from the pancreas itself, and a related infection.

Because my hospital stay was much longer than expected and blood was being drawn daily, it was suggested that I have a PICC line placed, as the veins in my arms were becoming more and more difficult to access. A PICC line is a peripherally inserted central catheter, a long, thin tube inserted through a vein in the arm or chest and guided to larger veins near the heart. This eliminated the need for repeated needle sticks, as blood could be drawn directly from the line.

How was I able to remain in a hospital bed for so long? There were times, as my recovery stabilized, when I would pull out my phone or laptop and respond to emails or do a small amount of work. That helped me feel more normal and connected to life outside the hospital.

I have since reviewed most of my chart notes from my stay at the Mayo Clinic. One note dated October 2, 2009, reflects many of Mayo's comments throughout my hospital stay: *"He has had difficulty with GI bleeding post-op as well as ongoing intermittent cramping abdominal pain. He has had two episodes of syncope, the last one being today that started when he had cramping in the abdomen. The prior one was related to GI bleeding."*

On day eleven, I also had a nasogastric (NG) tube inserted, a thin, flexible tube used to remove stomach contents and relieve pressure from a blockage. The ongoing challenge was determining the source of the bleeding. I also had fluid buildup near the pancreas and some hemorrhaging. All of this required careful management to resolve the complications and move me onto a steady path toward healing.

Mayo ordered regular lung and liver CT scans, as these are the most common sites where pNET cancer can spread. I do not recall ever being given a specific prognosis, either before or after my surgery. The same is true regarding long-term life expectancy following the Whipple procedure, except in the instances already mentioned in this book. I am not aware of any doctor's chart notes that contradict this. However, I did know the statistics.

The first time I recall being told that I would eventually need chemotherapy was in April 2013. Mayo's records indicate I was introduced to an oncologist on September 18, 2009, but I do not remember that meeting, likely because my focus at that time was simply surviving the recovery. I am thankful that chemotherapy was delayed as long as it was.

From the time I was discharged from St. Mary's until 2015, when I began chemotherapy, there were no treatments or procedures beyond routine blood work, CT scans, MRIs, and other monitoring tests.

Release from the Hospital

According to hospital records, I was in the hospital for twenty-four days. St. Mary's was my home until October 9, a Friday, when I was officially released from the hospital. We stayed in a nearby hotel for five additional days, as requested by my doctor. My last appointment was October 12th, a Monday, before I was approved to travel home. My progress and recovery were on track, and I was cleared to return home, which I did, arriving on Wednesday, October 14, 2009.

I still had several IV tubes in my abdomen, which made airport security and travel in general an unpleasant experience. In addition, our flight was delayed. I was uncomfortable waiting at the airport, and the trip home became long and exhausting. My stamina had not returned to its pre-cancer level, and this proved to me that I would need to rebuild it gradually over time.

Return to "Normal" Life

I did not expect to live a long life. For now, I was encouraged, and I felt better. Once I returned home, I slipped back into many of my old habits, eating as I had before, though with some limitations due to the removal of my gallbladder and the process of learning which foods made me feel well afterward. Learning a new habit takes dedication, consistency, and repetition, which can be very hard work. It is much easier to continue doing what you are accustomed to doing.

I lost close to thirty pounds during this period. Prior to surgery, I was the heaviest I had ever been. Kay and I later joked that God had fattened me up just so I could lose thirty pounds and not look like a bean stalk. I now believe that is exactly what God did.

I finally began gaining weight again after about two months and eventually regained roughly fifteen pounds. It was about a month before I returned to work part-time, and by early January 2010, I was working full-time again. The doctors had me try several enzyme pills, and I had satisfactory results from them. After several months, I no longer needed them.

I was also told that I would be pre-diabetic, which remains true today. My blood glucose levels fluctuate between high and very low. This imbalance occasionally causes side effects such as dizziness and feeling unsteady. I have been blessed to have relatively few food-related issues. Over time, as I returned to working long hours, I found myself largely back to my old, unhealthy diet.

Regular Follow-Ups at Mayo

My first return visit to Mayo was on November 11, 2009, a one-month post-hospital follow-up. At that visit, the IV tubes were removed, and routine imaging scans and blood work were performed. Everything appeared to be returning to normal. I did not know what to expect, as everything was a first.

It was a tremendous relief to have the tubes removed. Airport security always scrutinized me carefully because of them. During that first month of recovery, I rarely traveled or left the house. The tubes were the primary reason, along with the fact that I was still regaining strength. I felt uncomfortable being in public, even though the tubes were hidden beneath a bulky shirt. Having them removed felt like a major step forward, both in healing and in putting that phase of my life behind me.

Follow-up CT scans were completed at Sally Jobe in Littleton in February 2010 and again in September 2010. The results were sent to Dr. Kendrick for review. I traveled to Mayo in late September 2010 for a follow-up visit, during which we reviewed the CT scans and normal lab results.

Trips to Mayo were typically one to two days. This pattern continued through my December 2010 CT scan at Sally Jobe. Everything was healing as expected, my weight was stable, and my energy was returning. Kay and I began to relax and cautiously plan for the future. All reports either brought good news or showed no changes.

The next follow-up CT scan was performed at Sally Jobe on March 18, 2011, and the results were once again sent to Dr. Kendrick for review. I also sent him a letter on March 21, 2011, noting CT findings of spots on my liver. He responded by suggesting we wait to discuss those findings at my June 16, 2011 appointment.

At that visit, they switched me to MRI imaging. This was my first MRI. Based on all prior test results and reassuring comments, Kay and I decided that I could make that trip on my own. But that June 2011 visit broke the pattern. This time, the visit did not bring positive news.

- CHAPTER 7 -
STAGE IV: THE SECOND BATTLE BEGINS

The Devastating Appointment

Alone at the Mayo Clinic on June 16, 2011, for my follow-up visit, Dr. Kendrick used words that would once again change my life. Earlier that day, I had undergone routine blood work and an MRI scan in the morning, and in the early afternoon I met with Dr. Kendrick to review those results along with a CT scan from March 18, 2011, completed at Sally Jobe.

At my appointment, Dr. Kendrick told me, "Your imaging is showing indeterminate liver lesions. The largest is 1.1 cm. This represents a metastasis of your cancer to the liver that was not previously seen. We will need to see you again in three months to monitor these growths."

The stated diagnosis was: **Metastatic pancreatic neuroen-docrine carcinoma.**

My cancer had spread. (see Appendix E, Document 5 for medical documentation).

I was facing yet another devastating setback. I was now diagnosed with **Stage IV cancer.**

I did not know, nor could I imagine how much this news would once again affect my future. I knew it was terrible news. How would Stage IV cancer affect me? I already knew how grim the statistics were. How would I fight this, if at all? As I absorbed the news, my first thought was that I had to call Kay.

On that call, I wept through most of it as I shared my heart-breaking news.

The first time you are told you have cancer, you are filled with shock and many other awful emotions that are difficult to describe. The second time you are told you have cancer, whether it is a recurrence, relapse, or metastasis, is far worse. It is a crushing, overpowering feeling that sweeps over you, and you ask yourself, *When will this ever stop? Do I even want to fight this battle again?*

I returned on October 6, 2011, for another MRI and visit, followed by additional visits in April 2012 and April 2013. At, what would be my final visit to Mayo, in April 2014, I was told that I would need to start chemotherapy.

As mentioned previously, Stage IV pancreatic cancer means the cancer has spread beyond the pancreas to other parts of the body, with the liver being the most common site. According to available medical information, while exact records of the "longest" survivor are not readily available, some case studies report patients with Stage IV pancreatic neuroendocrine tumors living for several years, with a few documented cases exceeding a decade. The average survival rate for

Stage IV pNET is significantly lower, with most patients living only a few years after diagnosis. I fully expected my life to be dramatically shortened by this news.

At the time of my Whipple surgery, my pathology report was "clean," indicating no cancer was found in surrounding tissues. Twenty-five lymph nodes were tested, and all were negative. So why did my cancer spread one and a half years later?

Most of the time, we do not have a choice about whether to have surgery. That was my case. My tumor was large and had already wrapped around my superior mesenteric vein. Had it not been removed, it would have continued to grow and caused serious complications sooner or later.

Somehow, through effort and reflection on the previous years, I knew I had to find the strength and attitude to move through, and beyond, this devastating news. People often say that God does not give you more than you can handle, but those words are not found in the Bible. Learning that I had Stage IV cancer, I knew I had to do something different. As the old saying goes, *"Insanity is doing the same thing over and over again and expecting different results."*

In C.S. Lewis's book A Grief Observed, he writes,

> *"You never know how much you really believe anything until its truth or falsehood becomes a matter of life and death to you"* *(Lewis, 1961, p. 23).*

He emphasizes that true belief is revealed when the consequences are significant, when trust is tested in critical circumstances. This perspective encourages deep reflection on faith, because it is only then that one truly understands what they believe.

Dr. Chauncy Crandall, in his book *Touching Heaven*, discusses the difference between hope with God and hope without Him:

Fearful Hope vs. Fearless Hope

Fearless Hope is the birthright of every child of God. Fearful Hope describes the posture of many Christians who believe God can heal, deliver, and save and know that He sometimes does yet quietly wonder, Will He show up when I need Him? They hope He will. They beg Him. But deep down, they are afraid He will not. This kind of hope is wishful thinking; it is not the substance of faith. (Crandall, 2016)

After my second cancer diagnosis, I leaned even more heavily on my faith to help determine my path forward. In the next chapter, I discuss prayer and how sermons helped me stay focused and repeatedly turn to God, trusting that He was holding my hand through this dark time and would guide me forward.

My Mountain Prayer – A Major Turning Point

In 2006, before my cancer journey began, Kay and I purchased a cabin in Indian Mountain near Fairplay, Colorado, about a ninety-minute drive from home. After I recovered sufficiently from surgery, I spent increasing time there as I continued to recuperate. Sometimes I stayed alone; sometimes Kay joined me. Many special memories were made there with family, holidays, and gatherings, but it was also a place of solitude.

I would talk with God as I walked the land or worked around the cabin. It was a place where I could pray aloud without concern, as the area was remote. I prayed—and cried—freely, depending on my emotions at the time. At home, I missed those walks and private conversations with God. Praying aloud in an established neighborhood feels different when others might overhear or think you are talking to yourself.

Between 2010 and 2011, while still recovering from surgery, I watched many sermons from various churches. Occasionally, one would touch me deeply, as the ones I describe here did. I enjoyed the *Hour of Power* from the Crystal Cathedral with Reverend Robert Schuller, Sr., who preached powerful messages of hope. Some label him a prosperity gospel preacher, but I doubt those critics have listened closely to his sermons.

The Bible speaks often about blessings and rewards from God. Isaac, as described in Genesis 26, prospered greatly. Scripture never says believers must be poor. As long as money does not become an idol and God remains the focus, I believe prosperity is not wrong. What matters is what we do with it. Prosperity is not only financial. For me, prosperity comes from the promises found in my life verse, Isaiah 41:10.

A sermon that deeply impacted me focused on healing:

> *"Because you have so little faith. Truly I tell you, if you have faith as small as a mustard seed, you can say to this mountain, 'Move from here to there,' and it will move. Nothing will be impossible for you."* (Matthew 17:20)

The pastor said, "You have to tell your cancer to leave your body." I listened to that message again. The second time, one statement stood out: *Just as God speaks to inanimate objects and they obey, so can faith speak with authority.*

That sermon inspired me to try something different.

As I drove down from the mountain cabin, overwhelmed by the beauty of the snow-capped peaks around me, the words of that sermon echoed in my mind. I spoke aloud to God about my cancer and declared, "Cancer, leave me." I repeated those words again and again.

As I prayed, an uncontrollable smile, warmth, and joy came over me. The Holy Spirit came alongside me and said, "Yes, I will work on that."

I had no idea that this prayer would take ten years to be fully answered.

Diet and Lifestyle Changes

Coming home after my Stage IV diagnosis, I knew I had to make some changes. Kay and I implemented dietary changes in an effort to improve our health. There are many excellent resources available. One resource given to me by Dr. George Pardos was *The China Study* by T. Colin Campbell and Thomas M. Campbell. This study made suggestions for transforming the way I lived that might help combat my cancer.

One of the most important recommendations was diet, and to this day I continue to follow a modified vegan diet whenever possible. This means eating more chicken and fish while limiting red meat. If I do eat meat, I keep the portion small and increase the amount and variety of fruits and vegetables on my plate. I make a strong effort to limit processed foods, particularly "white" foods. I also learned about the ways lifestyle, attitude, and environmental factors play a role in maintaining health, each having the potential to influence cancer and its growth.

The growing body of research in this area is increasingly conclusive. Some foods and behaviors have been shown to help fight cancer.

Others may help hold it at bay, and some have even been associated with tumor reduction. These include whole grains, olive oil, flaxseed oil, organic foods, laughter, regular exercise, green tea, and certain herbs and spices. Cancer is a multidimensional disease, and therefore must be fought on multiple fronts—through diet, exercise, and a positive mental approach. I encourage everyone to consider these changes, even if you currently have no health issues. There is little risk in trying them and no meaningful downside.

Living with Stage IV: My New Normal (2011–2014)

Everything in life changes after learning you have cancer, and even more so when you are diagnosed with Stage IV cancer. It is a challenging way to live, carrying the weight of such a serious diagnosis. I was nervous and anxious and always prayed for good news, especially in the week leading up to any scheduled test or doctor visit. Through all of this, I never panicked or became overwhelmed. I kept reminding myself that God was in control, and I trusted Him for whatever comfort I needed.

One thing became very clear: living with cancer means living with the dread of the next appointment. You move from one doctor visit to the next, from one lab test to another, from CT scans to MRIs, always wondering what the next result will show. Will it be positive, stable, or negative? When you are told your cancer is stable, you feel immense relief, at least for a while. Then the cycle begins again, repeating the same questions and waiting for answers over and over.

Without my faith, and without God's promise from September 26, 2009, that I would get better, I do not believe I could have continued with an almost consistently positive and hopeful attitude.

At the time of my initial cancer diagnosis, I believed my faith was strong. Looking back now, after enduring this journey, I realize my faith was nowhere near where it is today. It has grown much stronger, and I know it will continue to deepen as I strive to live more fully for God and trust Him as I seek to fulfill His will for my life.

Throughout my cancer journey, I continued to work, ski, vacation, perform home repairs, and live much as I had before my diagnosis. However, I also added new habits: I changed my diet, prayed more frequently, and maintained a positive attitude. During this period, much of life returned to a kind of "status quo," which made it easier to stay optimistic.

Local Care Transition and Chemotherapy

At my Mayo Clinic visit in October 2011, Dr. Kendrick recommended that I meet with an oncologist who would eventually manage my chemotherapy when the time came. For nearly three years, there were no significant changes to my cancer, and my lifestyle remained largely unchanged.

That changed at my April 2014 appointment. The MRI showed an increase in both the number and size of the lesions on my liver. I met again with Mayo's oncologist, who informed me that I would need to begin chemotherapy soon to control the growth.

Kay and I discussed this new reality. We knew it would mean more frequent visits to Mayo, increased travel costs, time off work, and extended stays away from home. Because of this, we decided it was time to find an oncologist closer to home.

We focused on the University of Colorado Health (UCH) system, formerly University Hospital, because we had been impressed with the surgeon we met there in 2009. We found an oncologist specializing in pancreatic cancer at their Lone Tree, Colorado location, which was far more convenient than the main campus in Aurora.

Our first appointment with him in late April 2014 went very well. We were encouraged to learn that he was familiar with my Mayo doctors and that Mayo shared medical records with UCH. We felt reassured about the quality of care I would receive. The UCH Cancer Center had grown significantly since our first visit in 2009 and was now highly ranked nationally, both clinically and in research. Our new oncologist was well versed in pancreatic cancers, current treatments, and emerging research.

He was the first, and only, oncologist Kay and I met. After that visit, we knew we did not need to consult anyone else. Once again, God was clearly in the details, helping us find the right physician so easily. God was holding my hand.

Over time, this oncologist received several promotions and currently serves as Chief Medical Officer of Oncology for UCH, Division Head of Medical Oncology, Professor, Associate Director for Translational Research, and Associate Director of Clinical Services. He now practices exclusively at the main Aurora campus.

I began regular follow-ups with him approximately every three months starting in late April 2014. In January 2015, nine months later, he informed us that my cancer had progressed to the point where chemotherapy was necessary. He recommended Afinitor (everolimus), an oral chemotherapy drug used to treat certain types of cancers and tumors. I began this treatment in early February 2015.

When I started chemotherapy, I occasionally met with a nutritionist to help manage my diet and understand which foods were better tolerated during treatment. Certain foods affected me differently as my treatment evolved, and adjustments were made as needed.

CHAPTER 8

VERY AGGRESSIVE: THE DARKEST TIMES

My Accelerating Cancer

I was on Afinitor for about eighteen months. My cancer was monitored regularly during that period, and the drug was working. Then, in August 2016, I was told the cancer began growing again. The doctor told us that the typical life cycle for that drug was about one year, and I had exceeded that average by a few months.

My oncologist next recommended Lanreotide, a synthetic version of somatostatin, administered as monthly injections. The first shot was given in September 2016, followed by another in October.

The first injection came just before a mission trip to Kenya that Kay and I had planned months earlier with members of South Park Community Church (SPCC) in Fairplay, Colorado. Kay was understandably concerned that I wanted to go on this trip. She worried about my health, the distance from medical care, and whether I had the strength for such a journey, especially since I had just started a new chemotherapy and we did not yet know what side effects I might experience. But God told me to go on this trip, so I trusted Him.

We left for Kenya in mid-September 2016 and traveled to the Nairobi area. We spent several days in Mathare, one of the world's largest slums, working at The Inspiration Centre with Moses, the ministry leader. We were there to support the ministry, sharing Bible stories and teaching young children. Next, we traveled to Kikuyu, a small village, where we spent several days at the Children of Hope Orphanage. There we painted the walls of the orphan homes and again shared Bible stories and teaching. We were gone for about two weeks.

Some of the most vivid moments from that mission trip came from our time in Mathare. Each morning, as we waited for our vans to take us to the Inspiration Centre, young school-age children would gather around us. Over the four mornings we were there, the children began interacting with us more personally. On a couple of those mornings, as we waited, I felt a small hand slip into my own. It was one of the children's hands.

The picture was taken during one of those moments.

It was deeply moving and inspiring to connect with those children, even though we were there for only a short time. Mathare was a difficult place to be. Trash was everywhere, the smell of sewage was overwhelming, and by the end of four days some of us felt nauseated from the odor alone. Most homes did not have bathrooms. Along polluted rivers, charred oil drums were used to cook chang'aa, a potent liquor that is both a scourge and a source of income for many. There were no washers or dryers; clothing hung from buildings and rooftops. It was a hard way of life, if you can even call it that.

The children at the orphanage lived away from the slums, but they faced hardships as well. Despite their circumstances, they greeted us by singing to us, which was incredibly touching. A few of the children at the orphanage were physically or mentally handicapped. It was extraordinary to see how they had adapted to their challenges. One young girl had artificial legs, and watching her put them on was deeply moving, this was simply her normal life. When the children sang in worship, it was powerful and inspiring. Their songs were genuine expressions of praise to God.

This mission trip was a tremendous experience, especially spiritually. God's presence was evident throughout the trip. These children knew nothing different; this was their world. Many of their stories were both heartbreaking and inspirational. I loved being there, witnessing God's love and seeing His hand at work. It was an experience well worth taking. I believe many Americans are unaware of what life in a third-world environment is truly like. Kay and I both wished that our children, when they were young, could have witnessed these conditions, as it gives you a deep appreciation for what we have.

I returned home inspired by the children and with a renewed sense of gratitude for my life, even in the midst of cancer. I received my second Lanreotide injection shortly after returning. The following month, my doctor ordered an MRI to determine whether the drug was working. The MRI clearly showed that Lanreotide was not effective. In fact, the cancer had accelerated, it was growing extremely fast. My oncologist described my cancer as "very aggressive."

The Impossible Decision

Our oncologist presented us with several other treatment options. These included PRRT (peptide receptor radionuclide therapy), liver-directed therapies, liver embolization (cutting off the blood supply to cancer cells), and additional chemotherapy drugs such as somatostatins, octreotide, Lutetium-177 dotatate, and others. There were always new chemotherapy treatments being researched and developed.

Given how rapidly my cancer was progressing, my doctor recommended a chemotherapy cocktail that was being used off-label for pancreatic cancer. This meant it was not FDA-approved for pNETs and was still considered investigational. In 2014, this combination entered Phase II clinical trials and showed promising results. This discussion took place in late November 2016.

The documentation for this chemotherapy regimen included many pages listing potential side effects, most of which were frightening. At that time, my quality of life was still good, and I did not want to sacrifice it for a treatment that might cause significant suffering. We were uncertain whether this new chemotherapy would slow or reduce the cancer, and the potential side effects appeared severe relative to the possible benefits.

Uncertain about how to proceed, Kay and I left the appointment to discuss our options and to pray.

After many long days and nights of reflection, we returned to the doctor in early December and asked, "What if I choose not to pursue this new chemotherapy?" He responded, "Based on how aggressive your cancer is, I estimate six to twelve months of life."

Following that appointment, Kay and I decided to hold a family meeting. We shared this latest news with our children: the progression of my cancer, the treatment options, and the possible outcomes. We explained the potential side effects and admitted that we were uncertain how to move forward, and what choosing not to pursue treatment might mean. Our children were stoic, but there were tears—both theirs and mine.

For the fifth time in my cancer journey, I was facing a prognosis of less than one year to live.

Struggling with This Decision – God Already Knew the Answer

After our family meeting, we poured our hearts into prayer and had many deep conversations about the future. Kay and I once again discussed our options. Should we start this new chemotherapy, or should we leave my life expectancy entirely up to the Lord? I had been told, and I believed, that I would likely die soon if I chose not to begin this new treatment.

If we decided not to move forward with another chemotherapy regimen, I was at peace leaving my remaining time in God's hands. I had fought a good cancer fight for over seven years. I knew I had lived a good life, and I had no real regrets. I was as ready as one could be for my homecoming and to be with my God for all eternity.

As we continued to seek God's guidance, we soon learned His answer to our prayers at our next medical appointment. Hope, and a solution, were presented by God.

The Middle Path

At that next meeting, our oncologist told us he would support our decision either way. He then offered a compromise (God was there, holding our hand). He suggested administering this new chemotherapy, capecitabine (Xeloda) and temozolomide (Temodar), with the understanding that if the side effects became too severe, we could stop at any time.

For both of these drugs, regular monitoring of my complete blood counts (CBCs) and comprehensive metabolic panel (CMPs) were essential to detect any bone marrow suppression and to manage dosing appropriately to prevent serious complications. The doctor shared information about other patients on this same therapy and explained that, in practice, their actual side effects were far less severe than what the lengthy warning lists suggested. Only some patients had experienced significant adverse reactions. Based on that information, Kay and I agreed to move forward with these two oral chemotherapy drugs.

Capecitabine and temozolomide, even today, are still considered investigational for pNETs. In 2014 they entered Phase II clinical trials. In 2022, the FDA revised and updated the labeling to include pNETs, though technically they are still considered off-label treatments.

This treatment began very late in December 2016. The protocol involved two weeks on treatment followed by two weeks off, allowing the body time to rest and recover. Some of the side effects I experienced included fatigue, abdominal pain, nausea, diarrhea, blisters on my hands, sensitive skin on my face, chest tightness, occasional muscle spasms, and shortness of breath. Over the course of eight months, these side effects took a toll on my body, though many of them were manageable with additional medications.

Over time, the doctor reduced my dosages to help control the side effects. Quarterly MRIs showed reductions in the size of the lesions on my liver, confirming that the treatment was working. As time went on, my doctor sometimes without agreement from his colleagues allowed me to deviate from the standard protocol and further reduced my medication dosages. He also allowed longer rest periods to help my body recover more fully between cycles.

I believe God guided him in these decisions, allowing me to be treated differently than the standard research protocol. Otherwise, I am certain he would have followed it strictly. God had provided an answer to our prayers.

With each positive scan and each adjustment the doctor made, my outlook shifted, from a death sentence to a manageable treatment plan. This was a welcome "up" in the roller-coaster ride of my cancer journey.

- CHAPTER 9 -

THE LONG OBEDIENCE

Five Years on the Chemotherapy Cocktail

I underwent thirty-seven cycles of Xeloda and Temodar over nearly five years. Near the end of this long series of chemotherapy treatments, my regimen consisted of continuing to take the drugs twice daily, for two weeks at reduced doses, followed by five weeks of rest to allow my body time to recover from side effects and return to a more normal baseline. Even with these modifications to the treatment protocol, my cancer remained stable.

These medications have the potential to harm the body, sometimes doing more harm than good to the bone marrow, and they can lead to other blood-related health problems.

One great blessing throughout this process was that I never needed infusion therapy or radiation, nor did I lose my hair, and my side effects were tolerable. Prior to my diagnosis, when I thought of chemotherapy, I imagined sitting in a hospital or doctor's office for hours while medication was infused into an arm. I know many cancers are treated that way. For me, however, all chemotherapy was oral, except for the two Lanreotide injections I received earlier in my journey.

One unexpected change during this chemotherapy regimen was a significant drop in my resting heart rate. My oncologist told me, "You seem to have a new normal heart rate—mid to high forties, sometimes low fifties." I now regularly have to explain this to medical staff, as most people have a normal resting heart rate between sixty and one hundred beats per minute. A lower heart rate often raises concerns about underlying cardiac issues, such as heart disease. Because of this, medical professionals frequently ask whether that heart rate is normal for me. It is important to understand your own medical conditions so you can be a strong advocate for your care.

Life During Treatment

After the private equity sale of George's companies in September 2015, I officially retired in December of that year with a generous severance package. Within about six months, I started ZCG LLC (Zebarth Consulting Group), as I knew I still wanted to help businesses. My niche became helping clients sell their businesses so they can move on to the next stage of their life and goals. The firm grew steadily and has had several strong years over the past decade. I truly enjoy helping my clients with business challenges, taxation, and general consulting. This work provided both financial stability and flexible scheduling during my chemotherapy treatments.

I continued to live life as normally as possible, doing the same things I had always done—skiing, traveling, attending church, and participating fully in daily life.

In June 2018, my oncologist ordered a Dotatate scan for two main reasons: first, to confirm the presence of active cancer, and second, to determine whether I would be a candidate for future targeted treatment options once my current chemotherapy stopped working. This was a prerequisite for certain pNET therapies.

The Dotatate PET/CT scan is a nuclear medicine imaging test that uses a radioactive tracer (Gallium-68) to detect and localize neuroendocrine tumors. It is especially useful because it highlights tumors that express somatostatin receptors on their surface. My liver "lit up" on that scan, clearly confirming that cancer was still present and active. (See Appendix E, Document 6 for medical documentation.)

Not much changed in my daily life while on chemotherapy. With my first treatment, Afinitor, I experienced some side effects, but they were relatively mild. While I was on Lanreotide, I do not recall any noticeable side effects—that was the period when we traveled to Kenya. During the chemotherapy cocktail phase, I typically noticed side effects about three days after starting each cycle, and they would continue until roughly three days after stopping. These effects became more manageable as my dosages were reduced and as longer rest periods were added between cycles.

During active treatment weeks, I generally avoided traveling or doing anything overly strenuous. This pattern held true from late 2016 through July 2021. Outside of those treatment windows, I worked hard and continued engaging in all the activities I enjoyed. I love staying busy and active, and overall, my quality of life remained quite good, considering everything.

For nearly six and a half years on chemo, this became my routine. My attitude remained positive, even as chemotherapy took its toll on my body. Surprisingly, maintaining that outlook was not as difficult as one might expect.

Thank you, God.

Spiritual Growth on the Journey

During this cancer journey, I have had time to reflect on many things. One of those is how God works and the recognition that we do not know His ways. Why do we meet the people we do? Are we intended to help them, pray for them, or learn from them? One cannot imagine all the ways we have been changed, or how we might be changed, by someone we come into contact with. When is it right to pray for someone, and what do we learn of God's plan from each of those encounters? What is our possible effect on them, or theirs on us? This remains a mystery. We will probably never fully know how we have impacted someone, or how they have impacted us. God places thoughts in our minds; quite possibly, they are circumstances that He wants us to act upon or respond to.

Do you hear His voice speaking, whispering, or directing you? If so, do not ignore it. It is often better to act than to continue wondering. When God provides me with a command, I now try to obey Him, even when it may seem strange or awkward. That is often how God works in our lives. Sometimes His interventions are subtle and covert; other times they are unmistakably direct. At times He nudges us toward a new path He wants us to take. At other moments, He speaks in ways we cannot ignore, or plants an idea deep in our heart or mind. These are all ways in which we may hear His guidance and discern His plans for us.

I have experienced a number of these moments and believe I am now more alert to them. I try to listen carefully for God's voice. Sometimes His prompting is meant for that exact moment; other times, you may have days, weeks, or longer to respond. Generally, it is best to act quickly, such as making that phone call God places on your heart. It is deeply reaffirming when, during that call, the person says, "I'm so glad you called, I need prayer," or "You have touched me with your thoughtfulness." We must be willing to listen when God urges us to reach out or do something that may feel unusual at the time. Bob, a college friend, was one such person God placed on my heart. When I reached out, he told me the call was a blessing and that he needed it as confirmation.

Another example occurred in 2011. My employer was searching for a new electronic medical records (EMR) system. Jeff, a software developer with one of the companies we were considering, became someone I worked with closely. As we got to know each other, I felt compelled to share my cancer story. Jeff then shared that he had lost his sister to pancreatic cancer after a two-and-a-half-year battle, along with other significant family health struggles. A friendship developed. One day after we had skied together, he invited me to his condominium in Breckenridge. As I prepared to leave, he asked if he could pray for me. To my knowledge, no one had ever offered to pray for me face-to-face, one-on-one before. I said yes, though I felt a bit uncomfortable. We held hands, and he prayed for me on February 1, 2012. It was unfamiliar and slightly awkward, especially since I did not know Jeff well, but it became a moment in my life with lasting impact—one I will never forget.

When others know you have cancer, some will open up and share deeply personal or private experiences from their own lives. Welcome those moments. Embrace them.

My marriage to Kay continued to be strengthened despite all the challenges. For many people, life's hardships either deepen commitment or cause relationships to fall apart. Kay walked this journey with me, through the ups and downs. She was my rock, my true second opinion, and my sounding board. We prayed together and also prayed separately.

In November 2019, Kay and I took an incredible trip to the Holy Land with Rabbi Jonathan Cahn. We walked where Jesus walked. We saw where He taught and spoke with His disciples. We made lifelong friends on that trip, Ron and Wanda, and we cannot wait to return. There is so much to learn and understand about this sacred land and the Jewish people. Being in Israel makes the Bible come alive. Part of that comes from standing on holy ground, where thousands of years of history lie just beneath your feet.

We were baptized in the Jordan River, as Jesus was. We visited both famous and lesser-known biblical sites, guided by a rabbi who became a follower of Christ at age twenty after being an atheist, making the experience even more meaningful. One of the most memorable moments for me occurred near the Sea of Galilee, close to Bethsaida. The rabbi asked us to imagine Jesus sitting on a rock near the old church, teaching His disciples. He gave us an hour to reflect, pray, and envision that moment in history. It was surreal and overwhelming. I can still picture Jesus sitting there, across from where I sat. My faith was strengthened once again on that journey. Since returning home, we now watch the rabbi's sermons every Friday night and Sunday morning.

The Journey of This Book: Begun, Interrupted, and Resumed

While working for Madison Street Company, I often took midday walks during which I prayed and talked with God. In mid-2011, on one of those walks, I received the idea that I should write a book. At the time, I did not realize it, but I later understood it was the Holy Spirit planting that idea. Writing a book was never something I desired, enjoyed, or planned to do. Yet the vision I received was clear: I would write a book, it would be published, and I would travel to promote it.

By mid-2012, I had written about 15,000 words when the urgency to finish the book faded. I no longer felt nudged by God or motivated to continue, so I stopped, telling myself I would return to it later. The motivation to resume writing came again after my healing in July 2021, once more from the Holy Spirit. Even now, I can hardly believe the book is complete, just as God told me it would be in 2011.

Because I began writing in 2011, I was able to document the first two years of my cancer journey while the details were still fresh. Had I waited until 2021 or later, many of those facts would have faded from memory. During the years on chemotherapy, especially the chemotherapy cocktail, I kept meticulous records of each cycle, including side effects and MRI results.

I was living with pancreatic cancer, managing it, but I was not healed. I continued to seek God's guidance through daily prayer, reading Scripture, and listening to sermons from various pastors. Then Kay and I were introduced to a book study focused on healing, perfectly timed by God. He was holding my hand, guiding me toward sharing my journey while drawing me closer to Him. I continue to trust Him to lead me toward whatever He still has planned.

Embracing Spiritual Growth: Retreats and Revelations

In recent years, I began attending men's retreats. At these gatherings, we pray, share testimonies, and reflect on Christ's words. At my first retreat in April 2019, God worked through my meeting with my roommate, Stan. We quickly bonded over our shared cancer experiences. I attended additional retreats in 2023 and 2024, and God continued His work in my life.

The most profound experience occurred during a 4:00 a.m. encounter at the March 2023 Andrew Wommack retreat. God woke me and spoke clearly, directing me to write His vision for my life. The words came so quickly I could barely keep pace. Had I not been open to hearing His voice, I would have missed His divine direction and plans. These moments taught me that God desires involvement in every detail of our lives. Every whisper, every visit, continues to amaze me with His greatness.

- CHAPTER 10 -
THE HEALING

The Book Study – Early 2021

"Hear my cry, O God; attend unto my prayer. From the ends of the earth I call to You, when my heart grows faint; lead me to the rock that is higher than I." (Psalms 61:1–2)

Kay and I began a book study with another couple in early 2021, The Healing Light by Agnes Sanford. This book discussed healing, primarily the healing of others through prayer. I was skeptical, but I also knew miracles were real. I am proof of that. However, asking for—and expecting—healing was not something I was sure about.

Then one day I came across a Bible verse where Jesus tells the disciples, *"Very truly I tell you, whoever believes in me will do the works I have been doing, and they will do even greater things than these, because I am going to the Father"* (John 14:12). As I was listening to one of the Rabbi's sermons (after we had started the book study), I heard him refer to this exact verse when Jesus spoke to His disciples. Okay, I thought, now

I have heard this message two or three times, each telling me essentially the same thing. This repetition caused me to reconsider what I believed about the healing of oneself and of others.

The Prayer – January 2021

After learning more about healing and prayer through the book study, I began to pray and ask for healing for some of my extended family members. At some point, I decided to try it for myself. At least once, and perhaps twice, I said to God that I had restless leg syndrome (RLS), a condition that causes an uncontrollable urge to move the legs. It is a real annoyance, especially in the evenings when I am sitting quietly or when I go to bed. I also reminded God that I had cancer. I said, "God, if You could heal one of these, that would be great". I added that my cancer seemed under control and was not much of a challenge at that time. I promptly forgot that I had prayed this prayer and remained unaware for several months that God had heard and was listening. *"Ask and it will be given to you; seek and you will find; knock and the door will be opened to you"* (Matthew 7:7).

Liver Failure – February 2021

In February 2021, there were a few days in the middle of the month when I felt very poorly. I asked my oncologist what he thought, and he told me to wait and see what my regularly scheduled blood tests would show, as the blood draw was only two days away. Once again, God's timing was perfect.

When those blood test results came in, my oncologist called to tell me that I was in liver failure. Liver failure is a serious medical condition that often requires immediate medical attention, as it can lead to life-threatening complications such as bleeding, brain swelling, or kidney failure.

Many possible reasons for my liver failure immediately sprang to mind. My liver could have been damaged as a result of my original cancer; or perhaps the chemotherapies I had been taking for about six and a half years had finally damaged my liver; or possibly the cancerous growths on my liver were now causing significant impairment.

The oncologist scheduled a follow-up blood test for two days later. By that time, I was already feeling noticeably better, which gave me hope. The new results confirmed what I was feeling, as they showed my liver function levels were almost normal. However, the entire episode left me with questions: What had caused such a dramatic liver failure in the first place? And how had my body recovered so quickly? (See Appendix E, Document 7 for medical documentation.)

Nothing else out of the ordinary occurred during that time period, from January 2021 through early July 2021. I continued taking my chemotherapy cocktail, two weeks on and roughly three to four weeks off. I completed six chemotherapy cycles during that period.

The Voice

In June of 2021, I heard His voice. I was awakened from my sleep by a voice telling me, **"Ask your oncologist if you still have cancer."** I looked over at Kay and saw that she was still asleep, so I knew the voice was not hers. *Who said this?* I wondered. But the seed had been planted in me.

Later, I realized it was God, once again. I was truly *In the Hands of Our Heavenly Father.* He was holding my hand.

My next oncology appointment was just two weeks later, scheduled for early July. I never would have thought to ask this question, nor could I imagine challenging my doctor in this way. I trusted my doctor and the UCH MRI results. But now I had been told to question my cancer status, by God, who knows everything. I trusted God's command more than I trusted the doctors. When God tells you to do something, obedience matters.

The Question – July 19, 2021

My regular follow-up appointment (which occurred every three months) was on July 19, 2021. As we drove to the visit, I told Kay, *"If the doctor says good things about my cancer status, I will ask him the question God told me to ask."*

At the appointment, the doctor said, "Your blood tests look good, your MRI looks good, and your lesions are smaller and fewer than they were in 2015, when you first started chemotherapy. You have been on this treatment longer than anyone else I know or have heard of, almost five years." He closed his report by saying, "You are my superstar!"

That was my cue.

I said to him, "I have a strong faith in God. How would I know if I still have cancer?"

He looked at me skeptically and replied, "Well, one of your larger lesions is close to the skin, and we could biopsy it. Realize this would only assess one lesion of the many on your liver. If this one comes back benign, I will allow you greater treatment flexibility, but that determination would be based on only that single lesion."

We discussed the pros and cons of a biopsy and agreed to proceed. Our oncologist had told us at one point that a biopsy of one lesion is generally indicative of all the lesions on my liver.

The Answer – July 2021

The liver biopsy procedure was performed on July 29, 2021. Two days later, Kay, Zach, his girlfriend Sarah, Daisy, her husband Jeff, and I were having supper together at a restaurant. Note the amazing timing of this news, there are no coincidences. My family was all together to witness and hear what came next.

My phone chirped, and I saw the message was from UCH. I opened it and saw that the pathology report had come back. My eyes immediately went to the bottom line, which stated that the lesion on my liver was benign. I handed my phone to Zach to confirm what I was seeing. He confirmed that the lesion was indeed benign.

I then declared to everyone at our table, **"I have been healed; I am cancer free!"** (See Appendix E, Document 8 for medical documentation.)

"Therefore I tell you, whatever you ask for in prayer, believe that you have received it, and it will be yours." (Mark 11:24). I knew this outcome was not possible in any natural, earthly manner, but only through the supernatural healing of God.

This was the kind of detail that only God could orchestrate, the arrival of my biopsy results while we were all gathered around the same table. If that benign message from UCH had arrived even one hour earlier or later, we would not have been together as a family. Everyone at the table was genuinely surprised and deeply grateful. I believe my children initially thought this meant I was in remission and that the cancer was no longer active. They were understandably skeptical, as many would be, that I could be completely healed. Still, we shared a wonderful meal together, and they believed, at the very least, that their dad would be around much longer.

When I read the report, I knew I was cancer free.

Further confirmation came through my cancer marker results, which were nearly normal: lower than they had ever been, at approximately 400.

Throughout my cancer journey, my Chromogranin A (CgA) test results had varied significantly: 2,822 in August 2009 (pre-surgery), 1,602 in November 2014, 3,559 in February 2015, then a dramatic jump to 5,300 in December 2016 (when my doctor said, "your cancer is very aggressive"). By March 2017, after approximately three months on the chemotherapy cocktail, the level had dropped to 2,809. In March of 2022, it fell to 250. There were many CgA measurements throughout my journey, but this result further confirmed to me that I had been healed.

Once again, it took time to fully understand what had happened, but the puzzle pieces came together. I had experienced another miracle. In January, I had prayed to God to heal my restless leg syndrome, or my cancer.

During February, when I did not feel well, God was actually cleansing the cancer out of the lesions on my liver. Thus, it appeared as if I was in liver failure. Then in June, God told me to ask my doctor to prove that I still had cancer, which led to a liver lesion biopsy showing that my largest liver lesion was benign. God never stops working. God chose to answer my prayer from January. He chose to cure my cancer and not my restless leg syndrome (RLS). Nothing else can explain these independent yet connected events.

My oncologist discounts that I am cancer free. At one point, he said that the liver biopsy was taken from the wrong spot and that they must have missed the cancerous lesion. But this biopsy was taken from the largest of my liver lesions. I have not argued this point with my doctor. God knows for sure. I believe and trust Him. When He told me to ask my doctor if I still had cancer, He already knew the correct answer, and I trust that completely.

Why was I so blessed? I often ask God that question. Why have I been so blessed? I am a sinner like everyone else, and maybe worse than many. I do not know why I have been so blessed. Perhaps I am simply more aware of the daily and regular blessings I experience. I can tell you that, like most people of faith, mine has grown and changed as I have aged and become wiser. I am much better at giving my challenges, worries, and concerns to God on a regular basis. I used to worry about who liked me and who did not; now it is no longer important. I used to worry when people said hurtful things to me or about me. Now I find it much easier to let those things go. They no longer matter.

I had a serious diagnosis. Some people, when they receive such a diagnosis, move away from their Christian beliefs. Others grow stronger in their faith, while still others continue in unbelief. I believe these responses are similar whether the event is a serious illness, the birth of a child, the death of a loved one, or another life-altering experience. These moments can convince you that there is a God and that you need to seek Him. I turned to God. He told me in 2009 that I would get better, and I continue to trust His words.

Some may smirk when I tell them that I saw Jesus in the hospital. Why was I visited—not once, but two or more times—by Jesus? It is an excellent question, and I do not have an answer. My faith is not stronger or better than anyone else's. Perhaps I was open to it, or perhaps I simply recognized what was happening and did not dismiss it.

When I share my visits from Jesus with other Christians, no one has openly accused me of making it up or treated me as if I were exaggerating. In fact, one of my former clients found the story deeply uplifting when I shared it at his company's Christmas party. He asked me to retell the story at least three times that evening to his employees. Later, his wife shared with us a similar experience of Jesus visiting her in the hospital.

In our greatest times of grief, challenge, or struggle, I believe Jesus not only wants to comfort us, but actively does so. We need only open our hearts to receive it. I also believe many people who have such experiences are afraid of how others will react if they share something they cannot explain. Because of that fear, they remain silent. Jesus is with us all the time. I also believe in guardian angels and that angels are among us here on earth, helping to guide and protect us.

Last Chemotherapy

The final day of my chemotherapy, my "set free" day, was July 6, 2021, and that remains true today. As of May 2025, I continue to have lesions on my liver. MRIs do show some growth in two of them, which I declare to be benign. My oncologist believes my cancer is active again. That may be the case, but I continue to trust God and pray for His guidance in what I should or should not do. I have many options, and none of this changes my healing or this testimony. My oncologist has said, *"You will live a long time."*

Over the last sixteen years, I have spoken with many people facing serious health challenges. I often hear them say things like, "God, take this from me," or "I am scared." How does one respond to that? Their words reflect real fear. Every person facing illness or uncertainty will respond differently. My sincere hope is that this book brings you peace, comfort, or hope—whatever form that may take for you.

- CHAPTER 11 -

LIVING AFTER BEING HEALED

Understanding the Miracle

My pNET cancer was healed in 2021, and I pray this will remain true long term, although I understand it could return. Like everyone, I still have other health issues. I wear glasses, I recently got hearing aids, and I have restless leg syndrome. I have arthritis in my joints and benign prostatic hyperplasia (an enlarged prostate). To be honest, I rarely pray for these ailments to be healed. Having been so richly blessed already, they seem trivial to ask God to heal. Occasionally, I do ask for relief from my RLS, as it can be a real annoyance. I know God cares for us and shows His mercy continually, and He desires nothing but goodness for us.

Because of my healing, I now understand why I felt nudged to complete this book beginning in 2022, after stopping in 2012. God knew then that new miracles were still to come, ten years into the future, and He wanted them included in this book. He had me wait so they could be told. I believe God wants me to share His Word, His healings, and the truth that He is an awesome God. We are called to pray, to trust, to hope, and to receive what He has prepared for both me and you.

Throughout my journey, I never asked God the question, *"Why me?"* Nor did I blame Him for my cancer. Instead, the question I asked repeatedly was, *"Why was I healed?"* So many others are not, and I do not have an answer for that. What I do know is this: we must continue to pray, continue to believe, and continue to trust God. He carried me through my darkest moments and through many other times when I needed Him most. I often wondered, *"God, why have You blessed me so far beyond anything I deserve? What can I do to show You how thankful I am?"*

I remain in awe of my journey, from my diagnosis in 2009, to Stage IV cancer in 2011, to healing in 2021. What a journey it has been. What lies ahead, I do not know, but I trust God completely. After months of prayer, He revealed my path forward: He wants me to share His grace, glory, hope, and healings through this book and through my testimony, with everyone I can. He wants others to know Him, to believe in Him, and to receive His blessings as well. He is alive, He is active, and He is still performing miracles; and I am a living witness to that truth.

I believe this book honors my faith and praises God for everything He has done in my life, from my birth until today. I want to be His messenger, His vessel. I want to share how He has glorified Himself through me. He has truly been alive and at work in my life. I have described the many miracles and blessings I have experienced since my cancer diagnosis, and even before that. Those miracles and blessings are the reason I am alive in 2025. This is His story, about what He has done for me, so that I may honor Him by sharing it.

Continued Challenges and Health Issues

As mentioned earlier, I have additional health challenges related to my cancer and the removal of part of my pancreas. In late October 2015, I collapsed after a church service at SPCC and was unconscious for about twenty minutes. I regained consciousness just as I was being lifted into a helicopter for transport to St. Anthony's Hospital in Lakewood. I had always wanted to ride in a helicopter—it was on my "to-do" list—but I never imagined doing so strapped down, barely able to lift my head to look out the window. God answered my desire to ride in a helicopter, but next time I add something to my wish list, I will be more specific about *how* it happens.

A similar episode occurred almost exactly seven years later, in November 2023. I was taken by ambulance to Swedish Medical Center in Englewood, Colorado. Again, it happened as we were leaving a church service. Both times I knew something was wrong as I became lightheaded, unfocused, and unsteady. I was slightly more prepared the second time, but I still lost consciousness and fell to the ground. Thankfully, Kay noticed and was able to help ease my fall.

On both occasions, my breakfast had been waffles with maple syrup, very sweet meals that caused a rapid spike in my blood glucose. If nothing is eaten to stabilize it, blood glucose can drop sharply within one to two hours, sometimes below 50. Kay and I, along with my endocrinologist, believe this is what caused my reactive hypoglycemia (passing out due to very low blood sugar). Symptoms may include shakiness, dizziness, nausea, rapid heartbeat, and sweating. In severe cases, it can lead to fainting or seizures. Since I have been pre-diabetic since my Whipple surgery, I am more prone to this condition. A normal blood glucose range is approximately 70 to 140.

Tongue Cancer, Surgery, and God's Protection

In November 2024, I noticed a sore on my tongue. I assumed it was a canker sore and that it would heal on its own. During a routine dental appointment, I asked my dentist about it. He said I would not worry about it, but advised that if it did not resolve within a couple of weeks, it should be biopsied. When the sore persisted, I scheduled an appointment with an ENT (Ear, Nose and Throat) specialist. He told me the lesion appeared cancerous and asked if I would allow him to perform a biopsy, which I agreed to.

A week later, he called to inform me that the biopsy confirmed invasive squamous cell carcinoma. He explained that I would need to see a head and neck surgeon for treatment. This type of cancer begins in the thin, flat squamous cells lining the surface of the tongue and is often visible as a persistent sore. It is considered highly treatable, especially when caught early. Treatment options depend on the stage and may include surgery, radiation therapy, and chemotherapy. The ENT ordered a CT scan of my neck to ensure the cancer had not spread.

We met with three surgeons and ultimately chose one who worked at UCH. We knew he was a Christian, and he met every requirement we were looking for. The surgery would be a partial glossectomy of the tongue. To be honest, this cancer and surgery frightened me more than anything I had previously experienced with pancreatic cancer. This surgery could affect my speech and my ability to eat, even though the surgery itself would not be externally noticeable. One surgeon told us I would likely be in pain for at least two weeks and would not be able to do any client work, as I would be on pain medications and unable to think clearly.

The surgeon we chose was able to work me into his schedule and perform the surgery within about a week. Everything was moving very quickly, and I did not have time to fully process my feelings about this new cancer—which, in hindsight, turned out to be a blessing. On the day of surgery, we met a resident who was studying under the surgeon and who would actually be performing the procedure. It was also clear that he was a Christian. We asked about his faith, but he replied, "I cannot say more about that." We later learned that many healthcare institutions discourage their employees from discussing faith with patients, which I find very sad.

Had I not taken that early February appointment, I would have waited longer and worried longer. Everything about this trial unfolded quickly. Once again, my prayer was my Life Verse. I also leaned on two additional verses during this time: Genesis 50:20, which I referenced earlier, and *"And we know that in all things God works for the good of those who love Him, who have been called according to His purpose"* (Romans 8:28).

I realized that the enemy (Satan) was trying to stop me from finishing and sharing my book. In late 2022, I began having difficulty hearing out of my left ear. This was around the same time I started working in earnest to complete the book. After about a year of struggling to hear well, I got hearing aids to help. Then, in 2024, I was told I had tongue cancer. I was certain this would affect my speech. At that point, the book was nearing completion and was in the editing stage.

It became clear to me that the enemy was trying to take my hearing and my speech—the primary ways I planned to share my book and testimony. I knew I had to take a stand and I declared: *"Satan, leave me! I stand with God, and the harm you are inflicting upon me will only make my message stronger. Leave me, in Jesus' name."*

After surgery, about thirty minutes after I regained consciousness, I was able to drink through a straw. When Kay came into the recovery area, my tongue was still numb, but I was able to slur out a few words. A couple of hours later, when the surgeon visited and asked Kay how I was doing, I answered him aloud, saying, "I am doing okay." He looked at me in surprise and said, "You can talk already?" The very next day after surgery, I was back in my office, working on client taxes and business needs.

It was amazing to see how God had planned everything. For about a year, I had been wanting to sit down with Zach and Daisy and their spouses to share my faith story, to encourage them that God is real and to urge them to reflect on their own faith journeys. The diagnosis of tongue cancer created the opportunity to have that conversation. This clearly demonstrates how God had been with me throughout my entire journey. These events could not have been random or coincidental; God orchestrated them. Near the end of our discussion, I told them about my tongue cancer.

I was genuinely worried about this new diagnosis. How could this happen after experiencing so many blessings? I had to consciously return to my positive attitude and my Life Verse. Today, everyone tells me they would never have known that a portion of my tongue had been removed.

The medical terms used were superlateral border invasive squamous cell carcinoma, moderately differentiated. They removed a section measuring 1.1 cm long by 3 mm by 2 mm approximately the width of a pea, with the other dimensions much smaller, making the overall size comparable to a pencil-top eraser. I think I slur occasionally, but no one else seems to notice.

Not all of my prayers are answered, in case you were wondering. For example I still have lesions on my liver, I have prayed for them to be smaller, fewer or gone. I have been praying for this on and off since August 2021 to May 2025 (my last MRI scan). The purpose of my prayer is to further prove to my oncologist that I have been healed, as the liver biopsy proved.

A New Testimonial Ministry

I love to share my testimony about my cancer journey. I have given versions that last five minutes and others that last over an hour. When I shared a half-hour version with Pat and Pete, Kay's college friends whom we see from time to time when they come to Denver, none of us could have known what would happen just a few days later. Pat suffered a severe attack of pancreatitis and was hospitalized for about two months. She believes that hearing my testimony in November 2022 strengthened her faith, and helped her endure an incredibly painful and difficult recovery.

Kay and I have since reconnected with Pat and Pete and rekindled our relationship. There had been a period when Kay and Pat were not in close contact. God is so good. God was there, holding all of our hands with His wonderful grace.

At times I pray, *"God, make me usable. I want to truly serve You and Your purposes."* God has plans and dreams for us that are far greater than we can imagine, and I cannot wait to see them fulfilled. As one example, more than two decades ago Kay and I decided to tithe. It frightened me to think about how much money that would be. To our surprise, within a few months of making that decision, our income increased significantly. We were blessed, and we continue to be blessed. Our ability to give has been a blessing not only for us, but also for those who benefit from our tithes.

I have shared my pancreatic cancer journey many times. On one occasion, a woman who had heard my story spoke to me about her husband, who also had pancreatic cancer. She told me she always felt better whenever we talked. Her husband passed away several months later. At other times, people have asked if I would speak with someone they know who has cancer. I always say yes, but only a few have followed through and called. I know they are hurting and that they need someone to share their story with. I continue to pray for them, even if we never speak directly.

People often ask me for guidance on prayer: "How do I pray? What do I say?" I believe some assume I have a special or hidden formula because I have experienced healing and many blessings. I do not believe I say anything special in my prayers. I know I am a sinner and must regularly ask for forgiveness. To answer the question simply, my approach is to pray the Lord's Prayer, ask for forgiveness, thank God for what He has done and what He will do, and then pray for others who need healing, help, or God's presence in their lives. Each time I pray the Lord's Prayer, I emphasize a different part and reflect on its meaning. Occasionally, I pray for myself, just as I did in January 2021—a prayer that was answered and manifested within a few months.

I also reflect on several Scripture passages that guide and affirm sharing one's testimony. These verses speak to what God asks of us after we have experienced His work in our lives. *"But you will receive power when the Holy Spirit comes on you; and you will be my witnesses in Jerusalem, and in all Judea and Samaria, and to the ends of the earth"* (Acts 1:8). Peter and John declared that they could not stop speaking about what they had seen and heard. Paul shared his testimony before Roman officials and a king in Acts 26. Scripture also reminds us, *"But in your hearts revere Christ as Lord. Always be prepared to give an answer to everyone who asks you to give the reason for the hope that you have. But do this with gentleness and respect"* (1 Peter 3:15). Jesus Himself said, *"Even if I testify on my own behalf, my testimony is valid, for I know where I came from and where*

I am going" (John 8:14). These verses give me comfort and peace as I write this book and share my testimony, knowing that Scripture supports this calling.

Some people ask why God would allow my cancer to occur at all. I do not know, and I will not speculate. However, psychologist Dan Allender suggests that God allows us to walk through danger to reveal His glory and to experience the depth of His character. He teaches that suffering and struggles with sin reveal the profound love and goodness of God, drawing us closer to Him and deepening our dependence on His protection and guidance.

From time to time, I reflect on my life and ponder the many "what if" questions. What if my first job had not been in Iowa City? Would I have adopted Don and Brian as sons? What if I had not divorced Karen? What would our lives have been like? What if I had attended a local college near Pecatonica? Would my mother have lived longer? Would I have married a local girl and stayed in a rural setting? What if I had never met Kay? Would we have our three precious children? The "what ifs" could go on endlessly. I do not believe in luck. I believe God is in every detail, and He knows every day of my life and every plan He will bring to fruition. It is miraculous to consider how different life might have been if even one small decision had been made differently. I am deeply blessed and thankful for life as it is, not as it could have been or as I once imagined it might be.

Almost every day, I am amazed by how present God is in the details of our lives. I will share one recent example. I hired a local editor, Chris, to refine this book, helping with punctuation, word choice, added detail, and much more. I began working with Chris in August 2024. In late September 2025, he left me an audio message saying he had completed his work and was unsure whether there was anything more he could contribute. He left that message on a Friday, but I did not listen to it until Monday. That same Friday, I signed an agreement to begin working with Spirit Media, a significant next step forward. I did not realize until three days later that Chris had completed his work on the exact same day I engaged Spirit Media. Who but God could orchestrate such timing? God truly is in the details.

God Has Been Faithful

When I reflect, I do not know how I actually got through those challenging cancer days, weeks, months, and eventually many years. Somehow, I accepted it without much fear or anguish. I continued to put one foot forward each day. However, I know there were times, especially early on, when I cried out to God to help me deal with my disease. That year, 2009, is somewhat of a blur and feels like a lifetime ago. Kay and I did what we had to do to keep moving forward. So much has happened in my life since then.

I seem to hear the Holy Spirit more often lately. I wonder how many times I may have missed Him before, not realizing it was Him speaking. If you think you hear His voice and wonder whether a thought is your own or from the Holy Spirit, one helpful test is to look to the Bible. If it aligns with Scripture, then the message is likely from God. Everything is better when we know God is right beside us.

At times I ask myself, *Is what I have written real? Could I have made this up?* But when I put all the pieces together, I know that anyone who studies this journey will reach the same conclusion I have. It is very real and only possible by the supernatural hand of God. I occasionally revisit this timeline to reassure myself of that truth, it helps anchor my faith.

A Timeline of God's Faithfulness

Late July 2009 – I was told by a pathologist that I had adenocarcinoma.

August 5, 2009 – Ten days later, based on blood tests, imaging, and cancer markers, I was told it was a pNET.

Mid-September 2009 – Final surgical pathology confirmed pNET cancer.

June 2011 – I was told I had Stage IV cancer.

Mid-2011 – I prayed for God to take away my cancer while driving home from the mountains. I felt an overwhelming sense of warmth, peace, and God's promise to work on it. *I did not know it would take so long.*

Late 2016 – I was told my cancer was very aggressive and that without chemotherapy my life expectancy was less than one year.

Early 2021 – I participated in a book study focused on healing.

Late January 2021 – I prayed for God to heal either my cancer or my restless leg syndrome.

February 2021 – My doctor told me I was in liver failure.

June 2021 – I awoke to a voice saying, *"Ask your doctor if you still have cancer."*

July 2021 – I asked my oncologist that question.

Late July 2021 – I underwent a liver biopsy.

July 2021 – The biopsy came back benign.

I declared, *I am cancer free. I have been healed by God.*

Since July 2021, I have not had chemotherapy.

This timeline demonstrates that these events could not be random. It could only be God. God carefully planned each detail. No human—certainly not me, and not my doctors—could have orchestrated this. This was not coincidence. *"Your will be done,"* from the Lord's Prayer (Matthew 6:9–13), was fulfilled.

About five months passed before I realized that God had answered my January 2021 prayer. And it was ten years after my 2011 mountain prayer asking God to take away my cancer. This proves that we should never give up. As Scripture reminds us:

> *"Rejoice always, pray continually, give thanks in all circumstances; for this is God's will for you in Christ Jesus"* (1 Thessalonians 5:16–18).

We must pray continually.

Some state that chemotherapy was responsible for my cure or healing. I absolutely believe it helped. However, God led us to our doctor, and our doctor had the knowledge to know the best way to treat my cancer. I believe God imbued him with wisdom and discernment to treat my cancer differently than others, giving him the expertise necessary to do so. Chemotherapy itself is not a cure, and no one claims that it is; it is meant to slow cancer or, in some cases, place it into remission.

How did I develop and maintain my faith in God? I can only speculate, as I do not remember a time when I lacked faith. In my early years, my faith came from going to church, Sunday school, and confirmation classes. It was founded largely on a fear of God. That is what pastors taught and what I heard. I believed fear meant being afraid of God. I also heard that if you were not good enough, or did not do enough good deeds, you would go to that dark, evil place called Hell, and I knew I did not want to go there. So I worried. Was I good enough?

I later learned what "fear of God" truly means. It means having deep respect and awe for God. It means having a reverence of His majesty and power.

I do not remember a time when I did not have at least some faith; I was always a Christian. However, I never had a single defining "born again" moment like some people do. My faith and beliefs have grown and changed over the years. It also strengthened my faith to grow up in a town where almost everyone attended church. That shared belief created a sense of support, and the small-town atmosphere provided a bedrock for faith. Belief in God was simply part of everyday life.

My parents also shaped my faith. They modeled a Christian way of living, loving, caring and helping others in need even though it was not always clear how explicitly they believed in Jesus.

In my early years, going to church was on autopilot. It was simply something I did. While in college, I attended a Methodist church on campus once or twice a month. Many of the sermons were very abstract, and I often left without understanding what had been taught. Many of my dorm friends were Catholic and attended Mass every Sunday. I cannot recall us ever discussing our faiths during those years, which surprises me now. My faith remained mostly unchanged: I believed in God, and that was that.

Sometime around 2005, I realized that each of us can have a personal relationship with God. What a wonderful discovery it was to know that I could talk to my Lord intimately. You can speak directly to Him anytime, just as you would with your earthly father. You do not need to work to earn God's love, nor can you. He has already given His love freely; we only need to accept it.

I struggled with this concept for a while. All of us are on a journey, and it is on this journey that we try to follow God and His ways. We will frequently fail, and that is okay. We must keep trying. God knows us, and He calls us by name. Over time, I unlearned some things I was taught in my youth and even into early adulthood. I realized that some theology I had been taught was not biblical. I do not know why the churches I attended did not emphasize this Good News, it is clearly in the Bible.

God has had a major presence in my life, which I am sure is obvious by now. Here are a few observations for you to consider. You cannot see the wind, yet you feel it and know it is real. I never met George Washington or Abraham Lincoln, yet I believe they were real because of written records, eyewitness accounts, and history. Why, then, do some struggle to believe in Jesus? The same evidence exists for Him. Jesus said, *"Because you have seen me, you have believed; blessed are those who have not seen and yet have believed"* (John 20:29).

God works in many ways, even through painful events. My sister Mary had become a recluse and rarely accepted calls from me. Often, if she answered, she would hang up. When I visited, about half the time she would not answer the door at all. In the summer of 2023, Mary collapsed in her home and was found on the floor. Her son, Myron, called me to share the news. We had not communicated in a long time, but it was good to hear from him. Mary did not recover and died a few weeks later.

Her death was tragic, but it led to a renewed relationship between Myron and me. Now we talk or text from time to time. You never know how God's plans will unfold, even through the passing of a loved one.

Looking Forward

As I have mentioned, I was given a death sentence at least five times. When I think about how deadly pancreatic cancer is, and that I am still alive today in 2025, I know I am extraordinarily blessed, a living miracle. Kay calls me her "miracle man."

I am now in my sixteenth year of life after diagnosis. I am living a full and abundant life, loving God more and more each day. I look forward to what God has already spoken to me and to what the next chapter will bring.

Closing – Hope

I could not have imagined the journey I would take or how I would endure all those challenging days, weeks, months, and years. I accepted cancer, somehow, without much fear or anguish. I continued to put one foot forward each day. Still, I know there were times, especially early on, when I cried out to God for help so I could better deal with my disease. The year I was diagnosed, 2009, marked a steep drop in the roller coaster ride of my cancer journey. It seems like a lifetime ago. Kay and I did what we had to do to keep moving forward.

I walk closer with God than ever before, and yet I still fail every day. I have come a long way, but I still have far to go. I do not know why I was healed when others were not. I do know I have received far more than I deserve. Much like the song *I Can Only Imagine* referenced at the beginning of this book, these excerpts from another song feel fitting as I close. The song is *Goodness of God* by Bethel Music, sung by Jenn Johnson:

"I love You, Lord, for Your mercy never fails me.
All my days I've been held in Your hands.
From the moment that I wake up, until I lay my head,
I will sing of the goodness of God.
'Cause all my life You have been faithful,
And all my life You have been so, so good.
With every breath that I am able,
I will sing of the goodness of God.
I love Your voice, You have led me through the fire.
In the darkest night, You are close like no other.
I've known You as a Father, I've known You as a friend,
And I have lived in the goodness of God."

- "Goodness of God"
(Bethel Music / Jenn Johnson), modern copyrighted lyrics

Another song that is very special to me is *Because He Lives* by Bill and Gloria Gaither. Josh Aaron does a beautiful rendition in both English and Hebrew. One verse and the chorus say it perfectly:

"God sent His son, they called Him, Jesus;
He came to love, heal and forgive;
He lived and died to buy my pardon,
An empty grave is there to prove my Savior lives!
Because He lives, I can face tomorrow,
Because He lives, all fear is gone;

Because I know He holds the future,
And life is worth the living, Just because He lives!"

\- "Because He Lives"
(Gaither), copyrighted

When we lose someone to death, we tend to speak of them in the past. Recently, someone shared a different perspective with me: when our loved ones die, they are actually **ahead of us.** That is such a powerful way to think about dying. When our life on earth ends, our life with God continues. I love the image of God holding us tightly to His chest and saying, *"I love you, my child."*

"In your heart you plan your life, but the LORD decides where your steps will take you." (Proverbs 16:9)

In episode 193 of the television show *Last Man Standing*, there is a scene between Kyle, a young man planning to enter the ministry, and Ed, his elderly business partner. They discuss how Kyle might reduce his hours. Ed jokingly says, "I'll sign off on that if you can give me an easy-to-follow plan that will get me into heaven."

Kyle leaves to think about the question. When he returns, he says something like this (paraphrased): *I don't want to preach to you, but I believe certain things are true. If you want to talk about them, I'd love that, but there's no simple answer. You deserve more than that.* As Kyle is leaving, he adds one more thought: *I believe one day I'll be in heaven. But I don't know how that could feel like heaven unless I know you'll be there too.*

Those words are incredibly powerful and resonate deeply with me. I have shared this message with others, especially when there is doubt about eternity. I want them there with me, just as I know you want your loved ones there with you.

God is real, and so is the Bible. Both must be trusted. There is a library full of books written about God; it is called the Bible. It contains many books, written by many different authors over thousands of years, yet it carries one consistent message from Genesis to Revelation. That message revolves around God's love, grace, and redemption of humanity, culminating in the person and work of Jesus Christ.

There were thousands of eyewitness accounts of Jesus before the crucifixion and hundreds after the resurrection. Scholars who study the Bible note that there are more than 2,500 prophecies, found mainly in the Old Testament. Of those, about 2,000 have already been fulfilled. The rest will be fulfilled when Christ comes again. That is a remarkable claim when you stop to ponder it. No other book can make that statement, nor has any book survived thousands of years and continued to speak truth, even today, to those who read it.

If you have not already, I pray that you will soon come to understand and believe that the One and Only God is our Savior. God's love for you is deeply personal. Strive to grow your relationship with Him. He is your Heavenly Father, and He wants you to share everything with Him. God is my confidant. Only He knows my deepest thoughts, prayers, sins, and challenges. I am so grateful that He is my Savior.

There is always hope, and Jesus is that hope. Whenever you need Him, all you have to do is invite Him into your life or ask Him to help you with a dilemma you are facing. Sometimes you must be patient for an answer, and sometimes the answer is not what you expected, or even what you wanted. At times, you may be tempted to dismiss it. The Holy Spirit regularly communicates with us: through a thought placed in our minds, an idea impressed on our hearts, or through the words of someone else, words that only God knew we needed to hear at that moment.

I believe God desires us to be like a stone thrown into a lake. The stone creates ripples that spread outward from the center. Those ripples continue until they touch something far beyond where the stone first entered the water. I pray that my story has touched you in a similar way, like one of those ripples, continuing outward until it reaches exactly where it was meant to land.

> *"Yet I am always with you; you hold me by my right hand. You guide me with your counsel, and afterward you will take me into glory. Whom have I in heaven but you? And earth has nothing I desire besides you. My flesh and my heart may fail, but God is the strength of my heart and my portion forever."* (Psalm 73:23–26)

I heard this message from Rabbi Jonathan Cahn. It is about our heart, but it is symbolic of what we must do in life. He said, "Your heart must keep beating. It strives to beat. It fights to beat whether you cry, sleep, laugh, or moan in agony. Your heart's one goal is to keep you going. This is the same choice we must also make." We must keep up the good fight and trust in, and rely on, God.

Martin Luther said that Christians do not merely wish for better things, but rather wait for them with confidence. He emphasized the importance of waiting on God's promises and trusting in His timing, as seen in his teachings on hope and faith. Another statement I heard recently, and one I love for its symbolism, is this: "God is always watching you. He loves you so much that He cannot take His eyes off of you."

Worth repeating again:

"Here I am! I stand at the door and knock. If anyone hears my voice and opens the door, I will come in and eat with that person, and they with me." (Revelation 3:20)

"But blessed are those who trust in the LORD and have made the LORD their hope and confidence." (Jeremiah 17:7)

Remember, invite God into your life. It will change you. You cannot say, "I think." You must say, "I know, and I do trust and believe in God." Praise God always. May God bless and keep you. Allow God to hold your hand, and help you, as He has done for me.

My Personal Message to Readers Who Are Facing Cancer

I do not know if you will be healed like I was. I wish I could promise you that you will be. I cannot. Some of my friends, family members, and others were not healed. We have lost people we know and love to this disease, and others to different dreaded illnesses.

But I can promise you this: God is with you. He will walk with you through the valley. He will give you strength for each day. He will provide comfort and peace that transcend understanding.

Fight for your life. Do everything medically possible. Change your diet. Think positively. Pray fervently. Build your support network. Find a verse in the Bible, or more than one, that you can call your own "life verse." But also surrender the outcome to God. Hold your plans loosely. Trust in His timing. Know that you are loved by the Creator of the universe.

Your life matters. Your story matters. Your faith, even when it is as small as a mustard seed, matters. Do not give up. Keep fighting. Keep praying. Keep trusting. If God gives you the gift of healing, as He gave me, tell everyone. Share that miracle. Give Him the glory.

That is what I want to do through this book. That is what I do every time I share my testimony. I am not special. I am just blessed beyond measure. I would love to pray for you or hear from you, whether it be with hands laid on you, or in whatever way I can be a help to you. I want you to feel and experience the power of God's healing and the great peace that I have found.

My contact information is provided at the end of this book for that purpose. Please share a comment or your own story with me, and tell me if, in any way, my testimony has helped you. My email and text information are also provided at the end of this book for that purpose. If you know of an organization or group with whom I could appropriately share my testimony, please let me know.

Thank you so much for reading this book. Please share this book with those who God brought to mind as you read my story. It may help and benefit theirs.

Praise God. May God bless and keep you.

—Daniel Zebarth

PART IV

KAY'S PERSPECTIVE: CANCER, A SHARED JOURNEY

What follows are Kay's own words, perceptions, and reflections on the journey we shared. As difficult as my cancer journey was, I cannot imagine what hers must have been like. The emotions and challenges she faced during that time were profound and relentless. She was away from home for an entire month while I was in Rochester, while Daisy remained at home attending high school. Kay does not like being away from home for extended periods, and I believe that, like me, she did not expect my life to last very long. If our roles had been reversed, I often wonder how I would have handled it. I am certain it would not have been with the same compassion, strength, or willingness she demonstrated.

Throughout this journey, Kay stood beside me as my rock, my advocate, and my prayer warrior. While I have shared my perspective on these events, Kay experienced this journey in her own deeply personal way. Her emails, preserved by my sister Barbara, along with her reflections, reveal a parallel story of faith, love, endurance, and God's faithfulness.

This is her story, told in her own words.

CHAPTER 12

FOUNDATIONS
OF FAITH

D an asked if I would share some thoughts and memories from the time he was diagnosed and treated for pancreatic cancer in 2009. I think of that season as one of the major bookmarks in our life story. We all have those bookmarks—moments that become reference points for everything that follows. They are like the rings of a tree: when a major weather event or significant occurrence happens, it leaves a visible mark in the growth rings of the trunk. Our disturbance, our growth ring, occurred in the summer of 2009.

In hindsight, God was already preparing me for this "growth ring." My Bible Study group began a new study in January of that year on a book entitled *Good to Great in God's Eyes* by Chip Ingram. One chapter discussed how great risks develop great faith. These risks become windows of opportunity for spiritual breakthroughs. Without them, faith can remain flat. They are moments full of potential, times when one may experience a supernatural miracle and encounter the power and love of God. As much as I desired greater faith, I did not want the great risk.

Dan and I had experienced the death of our first child, Isaac, in 1989. When thinking about life and the risks that are inherent within it, we usually make decisions based on our hopes and the anticipated joy that may come from them. We rarely weigh the potential risks. No one starts a family thinking their baby might die, yet sometimes that heartbreaking reality occurs. It was only after we endured that loss ourselves that we realized how many families face this kind of grief.

At that time in my life, my faith was not strong, which made the experience especially devastating. Yet during those months of caring for and loving Isaac during his short life, I instinctively turned to God, even while also exploring every possible avenue for healing. I didn't want to leave any stone unturned that might help Isaac. God's presence was there, even though I didn't recognize it at the time. I only realized it later, as I began to learn more about Him. Looking back, I can now see where He was present at that first major crossroads of faith. That crossroads became a real-life encounter with God's goodness and love, one that set me on a deeper path of faith.

In the years following Isaac's death, we were blessed with our children, Zach and Daisy. I also became deeply interested in reading the Bible and learning about God, motivated in part by the loss of our baby. In 1998, I joined a Bible study called Bible Study Fellowship (BSF). It was there that many small revelations began to unfold. Over the next nine years, as we studied much of the Bible, my understanding of God—and my love for Him—grew. His Word began to *speak* to me.

I also discovered that God often communicates through names and their meanings, which became especially meaningful to me. My desire to connect with God through His Word, devotionals, prayer, and study continued to deepen. The more time I spent with Him, the closer I felt drawn to Him. When that pattern of time with God was interrupted or neglected, I could sense myself becoming less grounded. Without it, a day could feel more challenging, demanding, or frustrating, sometimes filled with anxiety or doubt. But when I spent time intentionally immersed in His light and love, life's challenges felt less intimidating.

Through Him, I have learned to find peace even in chaotic circumstances. He is with us, and He loves us. He will see us through.

But how do you know that, unless you experience it personally?

Twenty years later, Dan and I found ourselves standing at the threshold of another crossroads when we learned of Dan's pancreatic cancer.

- CHAPTER 13 -

THE DIAGNOSIS

I remember the day Dan shared the news of his pancreatic cancer diagnosis. It was a warm July summer day at Westernaires. Our daughter, Daisy, had a summer show at the Jefferson County Fairgrounds. The first half of the show had finished, and we were just about to leave the indoor arena when Dan said he had something he needed to tell me. We stepped out into the sunlight and began walking toward the horse trailer. Along the way, Dan stopped, looked at me with tears in his eyes, and shakily told me that he had pancreatic cancer.

A cancer diagnosis is never good news, but at that moment, I did not understand the heightened seriousness of pancreatic cancer. I had no personal exposure to it, and my knowledge was limited. Although my heart stopped with the shock of Dan's unexpected words, my initial impulse was to comfort him and reassure him that we would get through this together. The news was alarming, but my immediate concern was Dan and the pain and fear I saw so clearly in his face.

Later that day, after we returned home, I began researching pancreatic cancer. That is when I understood why Dan had been so tearful when he told me. The reality was daunting. The information consumed my thoughts. We read the statistics and survival rates, and they were grim. The odds of surviving five years were very slim. Still, we focused our hope on being in that small percentage, the slim category of survival.

I remember a particular morning a few days after Dan shared his diagnosis. I was lying in bed, listening to the familiar sounds of his morning routine, showering, brushing his teeth, the muffled sound of the radio playing in the background. Suddenly, a deep sense of sadness washed over me. I became acutely aware that he was just in the room next to mine, that I could hear him moving about, that his presence was *here*, in this precious, ordinary space of our home.

I savored that moment. It was one of those rare times of clarity, when a simple, everyday moment becomes profoundly meaningful. Did I think about how life could change soon? Yes. And yet, in that stillness, I was overwhelmed by how precious those ordinary moments truly are.

Those quiet, uneventful moments of daily life, the background details that weave together the larger events—can be the most revealing. I became deeply aware of how much Dan meant to me and how much I loved him.

Just as Dan continued his daily routine, I continued mine. Although the news of his cancer consumed our thoughts, it did not stop us from moving forward. Life did not pause. Instead, it became fuller, overflowing with new concerns, research, and decisions related to treating Dan's cancer. We focused on learning everything we could about pancreatic cancer, researching medical facilities where Dan could be treated, making plans for Daisy during our absence, getting Zach settled into his first year of college, learning how to pay bills using Dan's online system, and addressing countless other details that suddenly felt urgent.

It was overwhelming and stressful, yet somehow we managed. We leaned heavily on our faith and on the support of family and friends.

I don't remember exactly how I came across a book entitled *Praying to Change Your Life: A Guide to Productive Prayer* by Suzette Caldwell, but it was the book I brought with me on our trip to Rochester, Minnesota, when Dan was scheduled for surgery at the Mayo Clinic. The author had herself been miraculously healed from an aggressive form of breast cancer. She wrote about her mother, who was a devoted "pray-er" and a role model to her as a child, someone who taught her never to put God in a box.

The book emphasized the importance of prayer, especially praying Scripture and identifying specific Bible verses to stand upon during difficult times. As I read, I was reminded of the old hymn *"Standing on the Promises of God"* (written by Russell Carter in 1886). That image, standing firmly on God's promises, became especially meaningful during this season of uncertainty.

Standing on the Promises

Standing on the promises of Christ my King,
Through eternal ages let His praises ring;
Glory in the highest, I will shout and sing,
Standing on the promises of God.

Standing on the promises that cannot fail,
When the howling storms of doubt and fear assail,
By the living Word of God I shall prevail,
Standing on the promises of God.

Standing on the promises of Christ the Lord,
Bound to Him eternally by love's strong cord,
Overcoming daily with the Spirit's sword,
Standing on the promises of God.

- CHAPTER 14 -
PREPARING FOR SURGERY

We arrived in Rochester, Minnesota, on Sunday before surgery to meet with the surgeon and have final appointments and tests on Monday. I remember going for a walk with Dan after we arrived, around a lake that was nearby. I brought this book with me, and we sat down on a bench and read from it. Its wisdom encouraged us as it spoke of the power of prayer and the power of God's Word.

"Spoken, Word-filled prayer has power and causes God's will to be done on the earth. It is the engine that advances the Kingdom of God on earth. The Bible says that He watches over His Word and that it moves swiftly to do His work. He is bound to answer His own Word. Whatever situation you are going through, pray aloud with the force of His Word, and your prayer will produce God's plans for your life in His way, in His time. Lend God your voice and watch His plans multiply in your life." (page 70)

Dan and I already had Isaiah 41:10 inscribed on our hearts, a scripture verse that divinely surfaced that summer not long after we learned of Dan's cancer. It is my husband's favorite verse and we pray it over him and so many others when they face challenges. The words are living and bring peace and reassurance when unexpected news threatens to knock you down and lose your footing:

> *"So do not fear, for I am with you;*
> *Do not be dismayed, for I am your God.*
> *I will strengthen you and help you;*
> *I will uphold you with my righteous right hand."*

We were already equipped with strong, specific Scripture to pray that September afternoon as we walked around the lake, pausing to listen as Yahweh spoke to us about the power of praying His Word. His Word does not return empty.

> *"As the rain and the snow come down from the heaven, and do not return to it without watering the earth and making it bud and flourish, so that it yields seed for the sower and bread for the eater, so is my word that goes out from my mouth: It will not return to me empty, but will accomplish what I desire and achieve the purpose for which I sent it."* (Isaiah 55:10-11)

As I think back on that late summer into fall timeframe during the initial diagnosis and the decisions we made, I recognize God's hand guiding us throughout. We chose to go to Rochester, Minnesota, for the surgery because of the reputation of Mayo Clinic and their level of experience with a complicated surgery such as the Whipple. Those were the obvious reasons, but there were other "quiet" reasons, remarkable blessings that were waiting for us to discover as we waded through this sudden storm of pancreatic cancer.

Dan speaks to and documents the major miraculous turn of events, from a diagnosis of the deadly adenocarcinoma of the pancreas to the rare, less serious neuroendocrine cancer of the pancreas. I recall those moments so vividly: the doctor calling Dan on the phone around 9:00 p.m. one evening to bring us "good tidings of great joy." I remember thinking that God pulled a rabbit out of His hat. It wasn't a magic trick, though. God had thrown us a lifeline.

We were out in deep water with the storm swirling around us. Although we hoped, prayed, and had faith that God would see us through this health crisis, that phone call broke through the dark clouds with a ray of hope for our family. As I think back on it, the lifeline was most definitely a miracle, but it was also the manifestation of God in our lives—among the billions of other lives. The realization that He heard our prayers and answered them brought such humbleness and awe.

The tide had turned. The waves of fear and uncertainty were retreating, and waves of JOY and LOVE flooded my heart. The awareness of how intricately He is involved in our lives brought such a wave of humility—the Creator of the universe, who knows us by name, loves and cares for us so poignantly and intimately. To "see" Him work in our lives was a life-changer.

May we all seek Him. May we turn back to Him. And may we not miss Him when those risks try to sweep us off balance. The birth of great faith is found in those moments. They might even be called blessings.

CHAPTER 15

THE DAY OF SURGERY

The most common access point to Mayo Clinic is by referral through your primary care physician or surgeon. Dan self-referred, which was rare in 2009. This meant we had to coordinate everything ourselves—gathering medical records, scheduling appointments, and arranging travel and lodging. We paid for our own travel costs, meals, and other out-of-pocket expenses. However, Mayo Clinic was in-network for Dan's healthcare insurance plan, which proved to be an incredible blessing.

On the day of Dan's surgery, we were finally in the pre-op room after waiting some time to be called back for preparation. This pre-op room was small and windowless, sterile and quiet. Medical personnel rotated through, each giving Dan specific instructions and information. It almost became comical, as each person noticed Dan's wedding band and informed him that it would need to be removed before surgery. Each time, Dan explained that he couldn't get it off because it was too tight. One assistant announced that they might have to cut it off, but added that there were some tricks the surgery team knew that might work before resorting to that.

Dan was finally prepped and ready, at least as ready as one can be before a major surgery like this. There are times in life when there are no choices; to get past something, you must go through it. As we waited for his turn to be taken to surgery, we were mostly quiet, lost in our own thoughts.

It was then that I noticed the distinct fragrance of roses, of all things, in that still, small, windowless room tucked away in the depths of the hospital. I asked Dan if he could smell them. He could, and we both wondered where the scent was coming from. A dear friend once told me that the fragrance of roses can be an indication of the essence of Mary, the mother of Jesus, being nearby. It is often associated with a divine presence, blessing, or spiritual experience. We were at St. Mary's Hospital, after all, on the 120th anniversary of its opening on September 30, 1889. My heart skipped as a sense of peace and hope wafted in with that heavenly fragrance.

The moment arrived for Dan to be taken to surgery. We hugged, lingering for a few moments, as we mentally and emotionally weighed this transitional moment. The attending nurse noticed that the wedding band was still stuck on Dan's left hand. Once again, remarks were made that it would need to be removed. Then Dan disappeared out the door and down the hallway, and I made my way to the waiting room.

It was some time before the surgery actually began. The waiting room had a monitor where family members could follow the progression of their loved one's procedure. My future sister-in-law, Robin, had driven up from Des Moines, Iowa, to keep me company during the long surgery. Not long after the monitor showed Dan was in surgery, an operating room attendant entered the waiting room and handed me a small plastic bag containing the intact wedding band that had been stuck on Dan's finger. Whatever magic tricks they used, they had successfully removed the ring without cutting or damaging it in any way.

Later that evening, after Dan's surgery, the surgeon met with me and shared how the procedure had gone, confirming that the cancer was a neuroendocrine tumor of the pancreas. When Dan was finally settled into a hospital room, sleeping and resting after this difficult surgery, a significant insight came to me. The removal of Dan's wedding band symbolically echoed the removal of the tumor. The surgeon had removed the tumor laparoscopically, using five minuscule incisions, rather than the large "bucket-handle" incision typically required for pancreatic cancer surgery. Similarly, the ring had been removed with no sign of damage.

In that moment, I wondered if the intact wedding band might be a sign that our marriage would survive unscathed through all the challenges life had brought us.

The rings of a tree can mark a notable storm during its life, yet the tree continues to grow. The wedding ring not only represented our wedding day, but it also marked this cancer storm. Our marriage survived, I am happy to report, and continues to this day. My faith grew as well, and it continues to grow, knowing with great certainty that God indeed is with us as we journey through life.

- CHAPTER 16 -

HOSPITAL VIGIL AND EMAIL UPDATES TO FAMILY

Throughout Dan's hospital stay, I kept family and friends updated through email. My sister-in-law, Barbara, saved these messages. Reading them now, I can feel the roller coaster of emotions we experienced—the setbacks, the small victories, and ultimately, the miracle of his healing.

September 15, 2009 – Surgery Day (Tuesday)

Thanks for your thoughts and prayers. We have such a wonderful family and friends. I think God sends us His angels through them. We are so encouraged by the recent new diagnosis. I am so humbled by God's direct answer to prayer in this situation. To go from the original pancreatic diagnosis to this rare form, which is treatable and possibly curable, is a miracle. It's as simple as that, or as mind-bending as anything I have ever experienced. I am so very, very, very thankful and awed by this. God does hear our prayers.

I know it will be hard, but we have already been so blessed through this. I just know God will have an incredible story for us to share on the other side of these storms we're facing. At least now we have a strong ray of light shining into those dark clouds. It helps tremendously. We have God and His legions of "angels."

Dan just got out of surgery about 9:30 p.m; I just talked with the surgeon, and he said Dan did well. The tumor was bigger than expected, but he got it all. He said it was the pNET kind—hallelujah! I almost kissed the man. I was so happy to hear that. Dan is still in recovery.

Thank you all for the prayers, caring thoughts, support, love, and kindness we've experienced through this. I can't tell you how much it means to me. Dan is equally touched by all of you. God has blessed us in *sooooo* many ways. We will be counting our blessings, naming them one by one, forever.

How prophetic these words were to become.

September 21, 2009 – One Week Later

Still at the hospital, but this is not unusual for the kind of surgery Dan had. He wasn't progressing and has had major discomfort from bloating. All the normal routes to relieve it weren't working, so they finally placed a nasal tube down to his stomach, which relieved it. He is feeling better and can sleep.

He also had a PICC line placed today so he can receive nutrients, since he hasn't eaten for a week. So today may be the day we begin to move forward. They just took Dan down for a CT scan. They want to see what the leak looks like in the stomach. The leak has probably caused his bowels not to "wake up" after surgery. Once they can assess that, we can have a plan to fix some of the delays he's been experiencing. Again, all very normal for these Whipple procedures, especially with the type of cancer he *had*.

September 26, 2009 – The Crisis

This was the day Dan experienced his visitation from Jesus at 1:00 a.m., a moment I didn't learn about until much later, since he was too sick to speak that day. I only knew that something terrible was happening.

Dan had a "banner day" on Friday, then on Saturday developed nausea, abdominal pain, hiccups that would not go away, and cramping. The doctors indicated that this was part of the normal process of the stomach needing to wake up and start functioning again.

What I didn't include in that email was the terror of that day.

I arrived at the hospital around 7:00 a.m. Dan was in pain and didn't speak much. As the day wore on, he didn't improve. The nurse reassured me that this was normal after a Whipple procedure. The fellowship team made rounds late in the afternoon. Dan was no better, but his discomfort didn't seem to be of major concern.

It was just moments after they left his room that Dan went unconscious. His unresponsiveness, paired with blank, staring eyes, caused me to panic—I thought my husband had just died. I ran into the hallway yelling for help. The team was still just outside the room and came rushing back in. As they bent over him, calling his name, Dan momentarily came to, before going unconscious again.

It was then that they whisked Dan off to intensive care. Dan's life hung in the balance with the discovery of internal bleeding causing a major infection. Blood transfusions followed. The waiting and uncertainty during those few days were the hardest of the entire ordeal.

September 28, 2009 – ICU Update

Thanks again for all your prayers! We are experiencing the results of those prayers today. Dan is feeling so much better. He even played a game of cards with my sister and me today.

The doctor wants to keep him in the ICU through tomorrow. His numbers are holding, and the right ones are slowly headed down (white blood cell count, kidney function, and blood sugar). As he can go the other direction so quickly, as we found out on Saturday, we are happy to stay in the ICU until he stabilizes.

October 7, 2009 – Continued Recovery

Dan continues to feel so much better. In fact, we moved out of the ICU last Thursday evening to a regular hospital room, where we have been since. He had another passing-out episode on Friday morning, but after getting cardiology on board, they figured out what was happening.

He is also eating regular food now, much to his liking. The doctors are watching his hemoglobin and white blood count (WBC) closely now. Those seem to be the key numbers to monitor as he gets closer to discharge. His hemoglobin was holding steady this morning, but the white blood count is going up, which indicates an infection.

Dan had another CT scan this morning, and they ended up placing a drainage tube. Hopefully, the WBC will go down now. The doctor indicated that we may be able to look at going home toward the end of next week. We are praying that there will be no more complications and that this one gets fixed quickly.

October 26, 2009 – Letter to Barbara

We are doing great. Dan is eating well these days; probably since Friday or so, he's seemed to pick up on eating without getting uncomfortable. That is good, since he lost about 25 pounds. He also seems to be getting a little more energy. He was talking about going to the cabin for the day tomorrow. We will see… I don't know how the bumpy dirt road will go with his recent surgery.

He has been working a little as well and plans to return to the office on Wednesday of this week. I'm going to miss him! I've had him nonstop for over a month! I am glad he's feeling good again and wants to get back to normal life.

We return to Mayo for a follow-up on November 11th with the surgeon. Dan will have the drain tubes removed then. He can't wait, they have become annoying to him, sort of like a chain on his belly. He will not have to see an oncologist, but the surgeon will follow him now and keep an eye on things. He doesn't have any chemo or radiation treatments, which is so wonderful. We truly dodged some bullets throughout this.

Dan's guardian angel has been in full uniform, battling and shielding him from so much. Did Dan tell you the story about his visit when he was in the hospital? Someone told us that the space between heaven and earth is so much thinner in a hospital because of all the life-and-death situations and prayers being said there. Experiences like Dan's are not uncommon in a hospital setting. God draws near, or at least we are more open to His presence, in our illnesses and hurts.

- CHAPTER 17 -

FOURTEEN BLESSINGS AND ANSWERED PRAYERS

I want to share some of those wonders that were waiting for us in more depth. Dan and I listed fourteen *Blessings and Answered Prayers* that we experienced throughout this cancer season:

1. **God's timing in the sale of Zebarth Advisors before the diagnosis of pancreatic cancer**

    In 2007, Dan felt a nudge from God to sell his firm and accept a job offer from his largest client. The timing seemed random then. Looking back, we clearly see God's hand orchestrating every detail. The new position offered superior health insurance, which ultimately saved us over $75,000 in out-of-pocket medical costs during Dan's treatment.

2. Brief pain to alert Dan that something was wrong

Only three days of abdominal pain, but enough to compel Dan to see his doctor. Without this early warning, the cancer might not have been discovered until it was too late.

3. An expedited appointment to see the UH doctor through Dr. Carroll's connections

When we needed to move quickly, doors opened that normally would have taken weeks.

4. Diagnosis changed from adenocarcinoma to neuro-endocrine tumor

The miracle that changed everything. A death sentence became a fighting chance.

5. No physical pain or discomfort in the time preceding surgery

Dan was essentially asymptomatic, which allowed him to maintain a normal life and prepare mentally and spiritually for what was coming.

6. Biopsy of the liver showed no metastasis

At our first Mayo visit in August 2009, this news gave us hope that the cancer had not spread.

7. Laparoscopic surgery versus open surgery

Though recovery proved difficult, the less invasive approach was ultimately successful.

8. The fragrance of roses in the pre-op waiting room

A divine presence at the moment we needed reassurance the most.

9. **Surgical biopsy results confirmed the neuroendocrine tumor, with no cancer in the lymph nodes or elsewhere**

Clean margins. No spread. These words were music to our ears.

10. **United Airlines accommodated us with revised flights and airfare**

As Dan's hospital stay extended far beyond what we had planned, the airline worked with us on flight changes without the usual fees. A small mercy that meant so much.

11. **Bill's experience with the Whipple surgery**

A friend from our church, Bill Dowe, had survived the same surgery years earlier. Knowing someone who had walked this path and lived gave us tangible hope.

12. **Caring, professional, and excellent nurses during Dan's recovery**

The specialized care at Mayo's St. Mary's Hospital was extraordinary. These nurses were highly skilled and knowledgeable about pancreatic cancer. Their compassion equaled their expertise.

13. **The removal of Dan's wedding ring**

The symbolism of this moment stays with me. Removed intact, just as the tumor was removed, with barely any sign of the surgery. Our marriage, like that ring, would emerge from this trial unbroken, and in fact, stronger than before.

14. A healed marriage

This cancer journey had a silver lining. We became a team with a common purpose. The struggles in our marriage before cancer faded as we faced this challenge together.

- CHAPTER 18 -
THE LONG JOURNEY

Dan's cancer journey did not end with his surgery and recovery in 2009. Over the years that followed, I watched my husband face setback after setback with remarkable grace. In June 2011, when he learned the cancer had metastasized to his liver, Stage IV, I saw his faith tested in ways I could never have imagined.

His phone call that day broke my heart. Dan was alone at Mayo for what we both believed would be a routine follow-up. When he told me about the liver lesions, I could hear the devastation in his voice. This felt different from the first diagnosis. This felt like the beginning of the end.

Yet Dan refused to give up. He changed his diet dramatically. He prayed more fervently. He kept working, kept living, and kept trusting God, even when the medical news felt hopeless.

In late 2016, when his oncologist told us the cancer had become "very aggressive" and that without treatment Dan likely had less than a year to live, we faced another defining crossroads. The proposed chemotherapy came with terrifying potential side effects. Dan's quality of life was still good, and we struggled with whether it made sense to risk that for a treatment that might not work.

I remember those conversations clearly the tears, the prayers, the long nights of weighing options. Together, we sought God's guidance, and He provided a path forward: try the treatment, but stop if the side effects became unbearable. That middle path brought us peace.

For nearly five years, Dan took an oral chemotherapy cocktail. The side effects were manageable, and the MRIs showed the treatment was working. We settled into a new normal, living with stage four cancer, but living fully nonetheless.

- CHAPTER 19 -
THE FINAL MIRACLE

In early 2021, Dan and I joined a book study with another couple on *The Healing Light* by Agnes Sanford. The book focused primarily on healing, especially the healing of others through prayer. Dan was skeptical at first, but as we studied together, something began to shift in both of us.

Around that same time, we were watching sermons by Rabbi Jonathan Cahn every Friday and Sunday. In one sermon, the Rabbi spoke about Jesus' disciples and referenced John 14:12, *"Very truly I tell you, whoever believes in me will do the works I have been doing, and they will do even greater things than these, because I am going to the Father."*

Dan heard that message twice from different sources, the book study and the Rabbi's sermon. He began to reconsider what he believed about healing.

One day in January 2021, Dan prayed something bold. He told God that he had restless leg syndrome and pNET cancer. He asked if God would heal one of them. The RLS was annoying and kept him awake at night. The cancer, at that point, seemed under control, so perhaps God would take away the RLS.

Then, in February, Dan's blood work showed he was in liver failure. His liver enzyme numbers spiked dramatically. We were alarmed, was this the end? But within days, his numbers returned to almost normal. The doctors were puzzled. We didn't understand it then, but looking back, I believe God was cleansing Dan's liver of cancer during those few days in February 2021.

In June, Dan was awakened from sleep by a voice telling him, "Ask your oncologist if you still have cancer." When he told me about it, I knew God was speaking. His oncology appointment was just weeks away.

At that July appointment, when the doctor called Dan his "superstar" and said everything looked stable, Dan asked the question God had told him to ask: "How would I know if I still have cancer?"

The biopsy of a liver lesion came back benign on July 29, 2021.

I was at dinner with Dan, Zach, Daisy, and their significant others when Dan's phone chimed with a message from the doctor's office. I watched Dan's face as he read the report. Then he looked up at all of us and declared, "I have been healed. I am cancer free."

At that moment, I knew. Ten years of stage four pancreatic cancer—gone. Not by medicine alone, though medicine played its part. Not by diet alone, though Dan had changed his eating habits. Not by positive thinking alone, though Dan maintained remarkable optimism.

This was God.

God, who had been with us since that terrible day at Westernaires, when Dan first told me about the cancer. God, who changed the diagnosis from adenocarcinoma to pNET. God, who sent Jesus to Dan's hospital room to tell him he would get better. God, who filled the pre-op waiting room with the fragrance of roses. God, who orchestrated the removal of Dan's wedding ring as a sign that our marriage would be healed. God, who walked every step of this journey with us—holding our hands, guiding our decisions, and ultimately, miraculously, healing Dan completely.

- CHAPTER 20 -
REFLECTIONS ON FAITH AND MARRIAGE

When I think back on this entire journey, from that July day at Westernaires to the benign biopsy result in 2021, I am overwhelmed by God's faithfulness. He was in every detail. Every appointment. Every test result. Every difficult decision. Every moment of fear, and every moment of hope.

Our marriage was not in a good place when Dan was diagnosed. We were struggling. Then the cancer diagnosis came and shifted our focus. We no longer dwelled on the things that divided us; instead, we became keenly intent on healing Dan's cancer.

From the moment Dan told me about his diagnosis, we became a team. We had a common enemy and a common purpose. We had to fight together, or we wouldn't survive, emotionally or spiritually, even if Dan survived physically.

Together, we learned to trust God more deeply than we ever had before. When you face the possibility of death, the superficial falls away. What remains is what truly matters: faith, love, family, and the presence of God.

I am grateful for every day we have together. Every anniversary we celebrate, both July 9th and July 10th, the two days we were married all those years ago in a comedy of errors that resulted in a courthouse wedding in South Dakota. So many memories of milestones since that wedding day, and so many we have shared since Dan's survival from pancreatic cancer.

These are gifts we might not have had. Dan was supposed to die within a year of his diagnosis. Yet here we are in 2025, sixteen years later, with Dan cancer-free and thriving.

This is not the story we would have written for ourselves. We would have chosen an easier path, one without cancer, without fear, without the valleys we walked through.

But I wouldn't trade this story now. In walking through that valley, we discovered that we were never alone. God was with us every step. And in facing death, we learned how to truly live.

My faith grew tremendously during these past sixteen years. I know—not just believe, but know—that God is real; that He hears prayers; that He intervenes in the details of our lives; and that nothing is impossible for Him.

I've learned that the space between heaven and earth really is thinner in hospitals, in moments of crisis, and in times of desperate prayer. God draws near to the brokenhearted. He meets us in our deepest need.

And I've learned that great risks really do develop great faith. That book study I did in early 2009, before we knew about the cancer, was preparing me for what was coming. God knew. He was already at work, already preparing my heart for the growth ring that was about to be added to the tree of my life.

- CHAPTER 21 -
A LOVE LETTER

In 2019, Dan attended his first men's retreat. I wrote him this letter, which I want to include here because it expresses what I've always felt, but don't always say out loud.

Dear Dan,

I am so excited for you as you attend your first-ever men's retreat. I know it will be a banner weekend for you, since God led you to sign up for it. He has a reason and a purpose for everything, and I know He will be intricately involved in every part of this—On a grand scale and in a personal, detailed way for you.

I cannot tell you how much it means to me that you are a husband after God's own heart. I did not know when I married you that you were, but God did. I think we were both diamonds in the rough all those years ago. How blessed I am to have the love of my life be a willing pilgrim of the Way, the Truth, and the Life. And because we are on this path together, we have the assurance that our journey together will be, always.

I sometimes think about all the wonderful reasons I married you: your handsome, rugged good looks with your dark brown, wavy hair and kind brown eyes (Mom always referred to you as her "brown-eyed handsome boy"); your hardworking nature and strong work ethic; your quirky sense of humor; your steadfastness through some major life losses and challenges already at such a young age. These are some of the reasons but the most important one, the one I treasure the most now, and the one that was not a main consideration back then, is your faith.

It has been the gold along the path for me. We have traveled almost forty years together, and we have seen and felt God's presence in our lives throughout those years. We know how He has been there every step of the way guiding, providing, comforting, blessing, loving, caring, hearing, healing, answering and we understand and treasure how God knows us, sees us, and loves us.

My prayer for you this weekend, Dan, is that your faith will become even stronger, and that God will reveal Himself to you in new and deeper ways. May this time be set apart for you to meet with and be still with Yahweh the Great I Am, Elohim, your Creator who formed and gave you all the unique characteristics that make you who you are, dearest Dan. I pray that your spirit will be at rest in Him in a way you may never have known before.

I love you,

—Kay

EPILOGUE: Standing Beside Him

As I write this in 2025, sixteen years after that initial diagnosis, I am filled with gratitude. Dan is still here with me on this side of heaven. He's actively working with his consulting clients, sharing his testimony, and writing this book. He enjoys life and lives fully.

Our faith is deeper. I've watched Dan face every challenge with courage and grace. I've watched him trust God even when the medical news was devastating. I've watched him maintain his positive attitude, his sense of humor, and his determination to keep living fully, no matter what the prognosis may be.

And I've watched God work miracles – both dramatic interventions and quiet mercies, supernatural healings and everyday blessings.

This journey has taught me much about faith, love, perseverance, and the goodness of God, even in the hardest of times. I've experienced the power of prayer and the importance of community and family. I now know what truly matters in life.

If you're reading this and facing your own cancer diagnosis, or walking beside someone you love through their journey, I want you to know that you are not alone. God is with you. He sees you. He hears your prayers. He knows your fear and your pain.

I don't know what your outcome will be. Not everyone is healed the way Dan was. We've lost friends to cancer over the years. We've wept with families who didn't receive the miracle they prayed for.

But I do know this: God is faithful and good, full of lovingkindness for His children. He will walk with you through the valley. He will give you strength for each day. He will provide comfort and peace that transcends understanding. He will work all things together for good—even the terrible things, even the things that seem irredeemable—when we turn to Him and receive His love and salvation.

Keep praying. Keep trusting. Keep looking up. Keep taking one step at a time.

God is at work, even when you can't see it. He was at work in our story long before we knew we had a story to tell. He is at work in your story too.

Trust Him. He is faithful.

And He loves you more than you can possibly imagine.

NAVIGATING YOUR CANCER JOURNEY WITH FAITH AND COURAGE

I wrote my story to inspire, encourage, and provide hope to others facing monumental challenges in life. I also want to share some of the practical wisdom I have gleaned from my own journey, wisdom that may be beneficial if you are facing your own battle with cancer or another dreaded disease. This includes practical guidance, such as what questions to ask your doctors, how to navigate insurance, and how to care for your emotional and spiritual health.

In this appendix, I share everything I remember that you might find useful from sixteen years of fighting my disease. Some of this information is medical, some is spiritual, and some is simply hard-earned life experience. Please consider Appendix A as a handbook, one I wish I had been given in 2009.

Who Will Benefit from This Appendix

I trust many readers will find this section filled with helpful information, for patients, caregivers, those newly diagnosed, and family members. This is meant to be a resource. Feel free to skip around, read what you need, and return as often as necessary throughout your own journey.

This appendix is part narrative and part bullet point list. In many places, if you mentally replace *"I"* or *"me"* with *"you,"* the content may feel more personal and applicable. I am happy to discuss any of this in more detail via email. My contact information is provided at the end of the book.

Section 1 – The First 30 Days After Diagnosis

When I received the phone call from my doctor following my endoscopic ultrasound of the pancreas, my world was forever changed. I had trouble making sense of what I was hearing and felt uncertain about what to do next. If you are reading this appendix, you may be experiencing something similar. While I do not have answers to all of your questions, I can share ways that helped carry me through those early days.

Know and expect that the first 30 days will be the hardest and busiest period.

- Your mind will race, and your emotions may feel out of control.

- You are likely in shock, even if you don't realize it.

- You are probably in survival mode.

Share your diagnosis with those closest to you first.

You will need their comfort, prayer, and support. As you gain clarity about your diagnosis and prognosis, you can share with others as you feel ready.

Telling your children

- When and how to tell your children depends largely on their ages.

- In general, children—especially those living at home – should be told sooner rather than later.

Spiritual support

- If you have a pastor, priest, or spiritual leader, consider meeting with them early.

- Their guidance and prayers can be invaluable.

You do not owe everyone an explanation.

- You may choose to wait before sharing with extended family or friends.

- Give yourself time.

- I kept my diagnosis to myself for about two weeks. Looking back, this worked for me, but I think sharing the news immediately with someone close to you, would be best. In fact, they should go with you to your medical appointments.

Begin researching your diagnosis—but do so wisely.

- Learn key medical terminology related to your condition.

- Understand that the internet contains both helpful and misleading information.

- Be discerning and cautious about what you read.

Start a running list of questions.

Write them down and add to the list regularly. Over time, your questions will become more specific, such as:

- How many of these procedures have you performed?

- How long have you used this approach or technique?

- Why should I choose you or this institution over another?

- What is the most likely outcome?

- How soon can I be scheduled?

- Will you personally perform my surgery or procedure, or will an assistant or resident be involved?

Maintain as much normalcy as possible.

- Continue working, pursuing hobbies, and following daily routines when you can.
- My demanding job provided a necessary distraction from constant fear and worst-case scenario thinking.

Give yourself permission to cry.

- I cried in my car, quietly in bed, in special places, and with my spouse.
- Crying is not weakness; it is part of grieving and healing.

Accept the diagnosis—but challenge it as well.

- Acknowledge the reality of what you are facing.
- At the same time, pray for healing and release from the disease.
- Hold both acceptance and hope together.

Attack this challenge on multiple fronts.

- Medical
- Emotional
- Spiritual
- Practical

Ask for help—especially from your spouse or closest supporters.

- Let others do some of the research for doctors, hospitals, treatments and logistics where appropriate.

- This lightens your mental burden and reminds you that you are not alone.

Expect your priorities to change—dramatically.

- Daily habits and weekly routines will shift.

- What once seemed important may no longer matter, and that is okay.

- You will need to find time for new medical appointments, tests, phone calls, and everything else that now requires your attention. This can quickly feel overwhelming.

- Seek out doctors and institutions that have experience with your specific cancer or disease.

- Your diagnosis may be common, or it may require specialists who understand rarer forms of cancer or complex conditions.

- Resources such as U.S. News & World Report rankings can help narrow your search for institutions with expertise in specific cancers.

- Healthgrades and similar sites can provide ratings and background information on doctors, including experience, patient satisfaction, and quality metrics.

- You will constantly be learning new and important information.

- Do not expect to know all the right questions immediately. Be sure to write the new ones on your questions list.

- With each phone call or doctor visit, aim to learn more— and let that knowledge generate additional questions for cancer centers, physicians, and other medical professionals.

- Two sets of eyes and ears are invaluable. One person may think of a question the other does not. Compare notes afterward and discuss your impressions together.

- Do not hesitate to call back or follow up as new questions arise.

- This is your diagnosis, your life, and your responsibility to understand your options.

- Remember, the ultimate decisions are yours.

- Doctors advise; you decide.

- After gathering your initial information, review it carefully.

- Rate options by importance and begin narrowing your choices to the top two or three institutions or treatment paths.

- Begin collecting and organizing your medical records, or at least know where and how to obtain them.

- This includes lab results, imaging, pathology reports, and physician notes.

- If records need to be shared with another institution, many hospitals can now access this information electronically— with your permission, which can save you time.

- With the help of your research and advisors, decide who you need to meet with next.

- Determine which specialists are required, what additional tests or scans they may want to perform, and how soon those should be scheduled.

- Timeliness matters.

- In many cases, including ours, much of this work must happen within the first two to three weeks after diagnosis.

Section 2 – Building Your Plan for Treatment

Everyone's cancer is different. You will need to understand the uniqueness of your diagnosis. The first days and weeks will likely feel like a blur. Your mind will race, your emotions may be intense, and you are probably operating in survival mode. During that time, here are some of the things I did that helped me.

- Allow time to come to terms with your new diagnosis.

- Some of that time should be spent alone, and some should be spent with family.

- Continue to lean on the resources of your family and friends.

- You do not need to do this alone.

- It is crucial to seek out doctors and specialists who can help you navigate your next steps.

- To some extent, you must **limit the amount of research** you do.

- The averages, charts, and statistics you find online are just data. They are not your case.

- In my situation, I was often on the far right or far left of the averages.

- In some cases, I was not even represented on the charts or graphs.

- Most major decisions are made within the first thirty days.

- You may have more or less time—be flexible. Slow down or speed up your timelines as needed if possible.

- Seek out and obtain **two or more medical opinions.**

- For me, "opinions" meant different doctors, different institutions, and different medical practices.
- Opinion "shopping" should include each provider's:
  - Recommended approach
  - Expected outcomes
  - Recovery times and length of hospital stay (if applicable)
  - Possible complication rates
  - Other treatment options and their associated risks
- Your questions should include:
  - Will I need surgery?
  - Radiation?
  - Chemotherapy?
  - Other drug therapies?
- Ask about the **expected prognosis** for each alternative, including:
  - Short- and long-term success rates
  - Risks associated with each option
- Consider whether a treatment is appropriate *for you*, including:
  - Your tolerance for risk
  - Known versus unknown risks
- Ask what **newer or emerging treatments** may be available.
  - This may include AI-assisted therapies, laser treatments, or other advanced approaches.

- You may need to qualify for a clinical trial, research study, or drug protocol.
  - In some cases, traditional treatment must be attempted first.
- Make sure you fully understand each option:
  - Medical risks
  - Personal risks
  - Potential benefits
- **Experience matters.**
  - If a doctor says they have done "a lot" of these procedures, probe for actual numbers.
  - Doctors and institutions are required to track and know this data.
- Every center will be different.
  - Each will have preferred protocols and differing opinions.
- What is true for one institution may not be true for another.
  - You need to understand your specific case and your comfort level with each approach.
- Each choice you make can affect your **quality of life.**
- Are you willing to accept a reduced quality of life, possibly involving months or years of chemotherapy or radiation, in exchange for a chance at longer life expectancy?
- Or would you prefer fewer treatments, potentially preserving quality of life, but accepting a shorter life expectancy?

This is an extremely difficult decision.

No one can guarantee the outcome of either choice versus the potential benefits for you, based on your decision.

- Your options may also be influenced by **financial considerations** and available resources.

- Cost matters. Most people prefer local care, but quality, value, and experience must also be weighed.

- If you must travel for the best care, consider:

  - Where you will stay

  - How long you will be there

  - The associated costs

  - Decide whether you should travel alone or bring someone with you.

  - A second set of eyes and ears can be invaluable, though it may increase costs.

- **Track and record everything,** including:

  - Appointments

  - Dates

  - Test results

  - What you were told and by whom

  - Recommendations and next steps

- Keep an up-to-date medication list, including:

  - Current medications

  - Medications you no longer take

  - Dosages and frequency

  - Vitamins and supplements, including key ingredients

- Maintain a list of emergency contacts, and ensure those people know they are on your list.

- Keep copies of power of attorney documents, advance directives, and related legal paperwork.

- If stored electronically, know how to share them when needed.

- Write your questions down before appointments.

- Make sure your doctor is on your side and is willing to support your wishes.

- The doctor should be your advocate and coordinator, helping you understand what comes next and why.

- This is increasingly difficult in today's medical system due to extreme specialization. Many doctors focus only on their narrow field and may not consider your overall health. Traditional family doctors are rare.

- Providers practicing Functional Medicine or Integrative Healthcare may offer more whole-person perspectives and many will offer holistic approaches, if that is of interest to you. (You can find them through the Institute for Functional Medicine or the Academy of Integrative Health and Medicine.)

- If a doctor treats you with a dismissive or uncaring attitude, move on quickly.

- Do not let insurance limitations stop you from exploring your best options.

- Medical bills can often be negotiated.

- Know the maximum amount you can afford to pay out of pocket.

- Working during treatment varies greatly. Consider:
  - Continuing to work
  - Taking a leave of absence
  - Using PTO or employer benefits
- Maintaining some sense of normalcy can be helpful.
- Be honest with your employer.
- Ask about flexible work arrangements.
  - Reduced hours
  - Remote work options
  - Depending on your age and situation, early retirement may be an option.
- Insurance matters greatly:
  - Health insurance
  - Life insurance
  - Disability insurance
  - Supplemental and long-term care coverage
- Review your policies carefully to understand what is covered.
- Balance coverage with affordability.
- Too much insurance that you cannot afford is also a risk.
- Finally, stay alert to what God may be nudging or whispering for you to do.

Section 3 – Fighting on Multiple Fronts, at the Same Time

Fighting cancer, or any serious disease, requires engaging on multiple fronts simultaneously: physical, emotional, spiritual, and mental. No single strategy is enough on its own.

Diet and Physical Health

Diet is an important component of better health for everyone, but it becomes even more critical when supporting your body in a fight against cancer or another serious disease.

Some changes that helped me and others include:

- Eating a more **plant-based diet**

- Significantly reducing **red meat and dairy**

- Eliminating **processed foods** as much as possible

- Learning about foods that may help fight disease, such as:

  - Whole grains

  - Olive oil and flaxseed oil

  - Organic foods

  - Green teas

  - Certain herbs and spices

  - Regular exercise

  - Laughter

- Start eating healthier **as soon as possible**

  - I should have started earlier than I did.

- Diet alone did **not** cure me, God did that, but diet supported my body through the fight.

There are many excellent resources on anti-cancer nutrition. One that influenced me was *The China Study* by T. Colin Campbell and Thomas Campbell, along with the companion documentary *Forks Over Knives*.

Reducing Harmful Exposures

- Decrease exposure to substances known to increase cancer risk.

- Cancer rates are rising, especially among younger people.

- This is often attributed to:

  - Increased consumption of refined sugars and processed foods

  - Changes in farming practices

  - Chemicals introduced after the 1940s, including pesticides

Reducing Inflammation

Chronic inflammation plays a significant role in promoting cancer by creating a tumor-friendly environment. It can drive cancer initiation, growth, invasion, and metastasis through pathways that promote cell proliferation and survival.

- While inflammation is essential for healing, persistent inflammation—caused by infection, obesity, toxins, or stress—can:

  - Activate genes that support cancer

  - Suppress anti-tumor immunity

◦ Make tumors more resistant to treatment

Lifestyle choices that reduce inflammation matter.

Lifestyle Choices Matter

Lifestyle factors strongly influence disease development and progression, including:

- Smoking

- Poor diet

- Lack of exercise

- Excess alcohol

- Obesity

Healthy habits—such as a plant-based diet, regular physical activity, avoiding smoking and excessive drinking—can drastically reduce risk and improve outcomes. Many cancers are influenced by **modifiable behaviors.**

That said, habits are hard to change.

- It is easy to fall back into old patterns, especially when your prognosis improves and you begin to feel better.

- I struggled with:

  ◦ Working long hours

  ◦ Not exercising regularly

  ◦ Poor sleep

  ◦ Inconsistent dietary habits

Learning new habits takes dedication, consistency, repetition, and hard work.

Prayer Is Powerful Medicine

Faith in God and the power of prayer matters.

- Pray Scripture over yourself.

- Pray for healing.

- Accept others who want to pray **for** you and **over** you.

- Do not be afraid to call out the enemy.

- Declare Jesus as your Lord.

- Command cancer or disease to leave in Jesus' name.

- Do not stop praying.

- Do not stop believing.

- Believe in healing.

- Give it time.

- Practice persistent prayer.

- Build a prayer network.

Although God sometimes seems silent, He still hears us.

- Trust Him even when you do not see immediate results.

- Know the difference between **faith and wishful thinking.**

- Accept God's will, but also believe that God desires healing.

Jesus taught that faith does not need to be large:

> *"...if you have faith as small as a mustard seed, you can say to this mountain, 'Move from here to there,' and it will move. Nothing will be impossible for you."* (Matthew 17:20)

And we can be honest with God: *"I believe; help my unbelief."* (Mark 9:24)

You have power in declaring healing, but you should also invite others to pray with and for you.

It is okay to question God.

It is okay to cry out.

It is okay to ask "why."

Mystery and faith **coexist.**

Strengthening Your Spirit

- Find a Bible verse that speaks to you and make it your own.

- Thank God daily for what He has done and for what He will still do.

- Make prayer part of your daily routine.

- Be ready to receive God's blessing or miracle when they come.

- Acknowledge fear, anxiety, and uncertainty.

- I knew God was in control and did my best not to live in constant worry about "what might be."

One of our greatest spiritual weapons is the Bible. It helps us counter the enemy when he attacks.

Scripture reminds us that this is a spiritual battle:

> *"For though we live in the world, we do not wage war as the world does. The weapons we fight with are not the weapons of the world. On the contrary, they have divine power to demolish strongholds. We demolish arguments and every pretension that sets itself up against the knowledge of God, and we take captive every thought to make it obedient to Christ."* (2 Corinthians 10:5)

Section 4 – Caregivers and Family

As I have said before, it is very important to seek help and prayer from family and friends. If you do not have family nearby, seek out close friends or consider setting up a daily or weekly call with family members or others who care about you. Remember, your family is on this journey too. Do not ignore them or dismiss their comments and suggestions. They are processing this diagnosis alongside you.

Many people genuinely want to help but do not know what to say. You may need to gently guide them.

Always respond kindly and with grace. I found these type of comments to be supportive:

- "I don't know what to say, but I can't imagine what this must be like for you. Please let me know how I can help."

- "What do you need right now, and when can I check back with you?"

- "I will pray for you. May I pray for you now?"

Tell people what you need or what would help you the most. If someone offers assistance, say thank you—and accept it when you can. If their offer is not quite what you need, respond honestly: *"Thank you so much. What would actually help me more right now is…"*

Accept help when it is offered, and even when it is not offered directly. Many people want to help but are afraid of intruding or saying the wrong thing. Give them permission to help.

Caregivers and friends can assist with many practical needs, such as:

- Accompanying you to medical appointments

- Driving you home after treatments or medical exams when you are unable to drive

- Helping with meals, errands, or household tasks

Your outlook and attitude matter. A positive attitude is very important, not because it denies reality, but because it provides strength and stability for you and those around you.

At the same time, caregivers must not lose themselves entirely in caregiving. Encourage them to care for their own physical, emotional, and spiritual health as well.

Managing your children's fears is especially important. Be honest, but always balance honesty with hope. Children often want your presence more than your words.

You may need long-term care. Understand that this can significantly impact those around you.

As circumstances change, share information with family and close friends so they can be prepared to support you and one another through the journey.

You are not meant to walk this road alone. Allow others to walk beside you.

Section 5 – The Long Road: Living with Cancer

How do you handle the emotional toll of going from scan to scan, blood test to blood test, doctor visit to doctor visit? It is not easy. This may be one of the hardest areas to offer guidance on, because it is deeply personal and different for everyone. For me, I trusted God. I lived life every day with hope—hope that tomorrow the sun would rise, and so would I—and that I would face that new day boldly, confidently, and with optimism.

How do you manage fear and anxiety, which are so individual to each person? First, know that it is okay to be scared. Fear does not mean you lack faith or courage; it means you are human.

Whenever possible, have a good work-life balance. It is so important, on many levels. I strongly recommend that, if possible, you try to work less and enjoy life more. Find ways to focus on other important aspects of your life and less on your disease.

Get dressed every day and go somewhere, do something you truly enjoy. Maybe it is a hobby you have neglected, spending time outdoors, or traveling. Purposefully living helps keep cancer from defining every moment.

Find the strength to move through and eventually past devastating news, whether it is current or still ahead. Take care of yourself. Maintain your dignity and your sense of normalcy, whatever that looks like for you.

You are a person, not just a patient.

Celebrate milestones, big and small (stable scans, good lab results, finishing a treatment cycle, anniversaries, birthdays, or simply good days). Seek out support groups. There are pNET-specific groups and many others that provide education, encouragement, and connection.

Some of these will have local chapters that will be near you. If not, they may have on-line forums or blogs:

- **NETRF** – Neuroendocrine Tumor Research Foundation

- **CCF** – Carcinoid Cancer Foundation

- **PanCAN** – Pancreatic Cancer Action Network

- **NCAN** – Neuroendocrine Cancer Awareness Network

- **ACS** – American Cancer Society

- **NIH** – National Institutes of Health

If or when a treatment stops working, know this: there will usually be another option. We rejected some options and accepted others. Carefully evaluate the risks, potential benefits, and side effects of each. No decision is easy, but each one can be made thoughtfully and prayerfully.

Help others, it will help you. Share your story with newly diagnosed patients when appropriate. Offering words of encouragement can often bring encouragement back to you.

Finding peace with your diagnosis is also very difficult. Just as important is finding peace with God. Healing does not always mean a cure; sometimes it means acceptance, strength, and perseverance through what life has placed before us.

Cancer can feel like a death sentence and can create paralysis. But for those of us facing cancer or any dreaded disease, we must fight and pray, and continue to fight and pray. Sometimes that may mean being alone on a quiet getaway; other times it means being surrounded by family, friends, and your church community.

If you do not have faith, I cannot stress enough how important faith and trust in God can be. Faith saved my life on several occasions—not only physically, but emotionally and spiritually. It gave me strength to fight every step of the way and to continue the battle, no matter how long the road became.

You are not alone on this journey.

Section 6 – Life after Cancer

What is the difference between being *"healed"* versus *"in remission"* versus *"cured"*? I do not know the official medical definitions, but remission is the easiest to explain. Remission means that cancer is still present, but it is not currently growing or spreading.

Being *cured*, I believe, is rare in the cancer world. You may hear this term used after surgery or radiation when a doctor says, "we got it all," or that surrounding tissue samples were "clean." That *might* mean you are cured, but even then, "cured" is a statement defined by time—often many years without recurrence.

Healing, as I define it, is different. Healing is a miracle from God. It is not the same as remission or being cured or even being cancer-free by medical standards. Could someone who has been healed get cancer again? Yes, it is possible.

We must remember that there is evil all around us. The enemy (Satan) loves it when we live in fear or when we do not fully trust God. The number one battle in our lives takes place in the spiritual realm, and it often manifests in our thoughts, emotions, and physical bodies. The enemy thrives when we say "woe is me," give up hope, or stop trusting God.

I believe that every cancer has the potential to spread and that everyone has cancer cells in their body. The medical community largely agrees with this, although how it is explained varies. For example, the National Institute of Health (NIH) states that surgery—while a crucial intervention—can also trigger biological responses that may accelerate micrometastatic disease. Research shows that surgical trauma can suppress anti-tumor immunity, increase circulating cancer cells, and induce inflammatory responses that may contribute to cancer progression in certain cases.

A typical healthy cell has a life cycle of growth, division, and death. A cancer cell is essentially the same cell, but it becomes abnormal. It no longer follows the normal cycle. Normally, cells with damaged DNA either repair themselves or die naturally. Cancer occurs when damaged cells continue dividing with errors.

In Western culture, research suggests that approximately 75 percent of people may carry dormant cancer cells that never become active. In the remaining 25 percent, those cells may become aggressive. Much of this information can be found in medical literature and reputable sources such as Healthline, Medical News Today, the National Cancer Institute, and the NIH.

Research increasingly supports the belief that cancer is approximately 15 percent hereditary and 85 percent environmental. Science has clearly confirmed that what we put into our bodies, and how we live our lives, has a major influence on our overall health.

Surveillance and regular follow-ups with your doctor are extremely important. God can guide physicians with wisdom and discernment in choosing treatments that are appropriate and timely for your care.

Dealing with *survivor's guilt* can be very real and very difficult. I have reflected deeply on why I was healed while others were not. The simple and honest answer is that I do not know. Only God knows.

Paying it forward through testimony and sharing your story is powerful. I know that I am called to share my healing story, through this book and through spoken testimony, with as many people as possible. I live my life now to help and encourage others, to share the message that there is always hope, that God is present, and that He desires healing for all.

Life after cancer is not the end of the story. For many, it is the beginning of a new calling.

Section 7 – What I Wished I Would Have Known

1. My Top Helpful Points to Consider When Dealing with Cancer

- **Placement of a Power Port or PICC line** I would have had one, or both, placed sooner.

- **More MRIs, fewer CT scans** CT scans involve significantly more radiation exposure.

- **A healthier diet sooner** I am convinced this is a key factor in healing and in simply feeling better.

- **Prayer is essential** I should have focused more on prayer earlier, asking God for help and thanking Him for what He had already done and what He still would do.

- **Professionally and politely questioning my doctor(s)** I wish I had asked more questions about treatment options and why certain approaches were being recommended.

- **Staying current on new and emerging research and treatments** Especially as it relates to my specific cancer or disease.

- **Don't fully accept when doctors are dismissive of vitamins and supplements** If they then strongly promote prescription drugs without discussion of collaborative options.

- **Obtaining supplemental insurance before diagnosis** This would have significantly reduced out-of-pocket costs related to travel, lodging, meals, and other non-medical expenses.

2. Symptoms for Pancreatic Cancer

- Dull pain in the upper abdomen, middle back, or upper back
- Pain in the center of the abdomen radiating to the back (my case)
- Pain that worsens when lying down and improves when leaning forward
- Jaundice
- Unexplained weight loss
- Unexplained fatigue

Hormone-Secreting Tumors:

- Low blood sugar, weakness, confusion, sweating — *Insulinoma*
- Severe ulcers, nausea, loss of appetite — *Gastrinoma*
- Severe diarrhea — *VIPoma*
- High blood sugar, diabetes, excessive thirst, frequent urination — *Glucagonoma*

3. Plan and Document Your End-of-Life Wishes

- This is practical advice, not meant to discourage or depress, but something that is needed no matter your life stage.
- Write them down and share them with your spouse or a trusted person
- I also wrote personal letters to my children, my sisters, and Kay

4. Other Considerations – Lessons I Learned

- **Knowledge about supplements,** such as Vitamin C. New research suggests that when combined with chemotherapy.

Pancreatic cancer survival increases and makes chemotherapy easier to tolerate.

- **Researched surgical options more thoroughly** I should have explored more thoroughly the drawbacks of laparoscopic surgery. I might have chosen the traditional "bucket handle" incision instead, which may have resulted in faster recovery and fewer infections.

- **Learned medical terminology earlier** Especially terms specific to my cancer and what they meant.

- **Asked more questions about cancer characteristics,** including:
    - Staging
    - Grading
    - Tumor size
    - Hormone-secreting vs. non-secreting tumors
    - Prognosis

In short, I should not have been afraid to ask more questions or request follow-up explanations.

5. Every Cancer—and Every Person—is Different

- Some people do very well with aggressive treatments; others do not.

- I wish I had stopped some of my internet research sooner and relied on a balance of asking informed questions directly to my doctors.

Final Encouragement and Thoughts

- **Attitude matters,** both medically and spiritually.

- **Maintain hope,** even when statistics or your personal test results are devastating.

- **Share your concerns from the heart** with family and others, as appropriate. Do not be a martyr or carry this burden alone.

- **Uncontrolled pain can cloud your thinking.** Address pain early and honestly with your medical team.

- **It is okay to have bad days.** You will experience moments of despair. Fight through those times and remember that God is with you, holding your hand.

- **Sometimes a simple prayer, a whisper, or a message from Jesus can change everything.** It may come unexpectedly. Be open to it, and receive it.

- **Find your own personal reasons to keep fighting the battle,** whether it is your children, grandchildren, spouse, or a milestone you still want to achieve. Focus on that reason, or those people, when the days are hard.

- **Continue to live life after diagnosis as fully as possible.** Do not give in to giving up. Push yourself, as you are able, to regain control of your life, to enjoy it, and to continue doing the things you love. This helps maintain a sense of normalcy and purpose. I continued to work hard, ski somewhat regularly, vacation, and take on projects I enjoyed, along with all the ordinary responsibilities of life. I planned around chemotherapy treatments as best I could.

- APPENDIX B -
PATTERNS OF GOD'S INTERVENTIONS

Appendix B demonstrates that my healing was **not an isolated miracle,** but rather part of a **pattern of God's intervention** over many years especially during the last sixteen years.

There are many ways God may manifest His presence. People describe moments such as these when they have sensed His presence:

"I had a strange sensation, an urge, and I felt it all over my body."

"My hands were tingling, and I did not know what it was."

"I sensed God in a way I cannot explain."

"I did not see anything, but He was there."

"I did not understand what was happening."

"I could not stop crying, or laughing."

"God was there with me."

Some of these mirror my own experiences and affirm that God continues to reveal Himself in deeply personal and sometimes mysterious ways.

In Robert Heidler's book, The Messianic Church Arising!, the author describes how people have moments when they felt God speaking to them, they were surrounded by His love, or felt the room filled with an unusual light. Others described physical sensations, warmth throughout the body, tingling hands, or an overwhelming awareness that God was present, even though they could not see Him. Some recall uncontrollable weeping, tears flowing freely, and a deep inner knowing that God was there.

A Pattern of Divine Intervention

Divorce Visitation – 1980

Context

I wrestled deeply with my divorce decision. I moved out of our home to reflect on what I should do and what I believed would ultimately be best. One night, I lay on the floor in my sleeping bag, weeping and agonizing over this major life decision.

Experience

Jesus appeared and spoke to me. He stood at my feet, small in stature, and His voice was soft and reassuring. He said: *"I know that you are struggling with this decision. It is okay to move on."* No one knew of my emotional struggle at that time. I had not shared my agony with anyone. After He spoke, He quickly left. I firmly believe He gave me permission to make a very difficult decision, one that had been a heavy burden I was carrying.

Impact

This was my first awareness that God would, or even could, communicate with me directly. I had never been taught this, nor had I heard about such experiences in Sunday School, church, or from others.

Connection

How might this experience relate to later whispers or messages from God? How could it connect to my cancer journey? This encounter gave me early knowledge, and some experience, to recognize God's voice, or at least to remain open to hearing Him speak. It also confirmed for me that He could speak to me again in the future, just as He could speak to others.

Scripture

"Ask and it will be given to you; seek and you will find; knock and the door will be opened to you." (Matthew 7:7)

Context

In late 2005, my largest client asked me to come work for him. At that time, I told him no, but suggested we meet again in two years. The timing was not right now. I continued to work and grow both firms, with a future transition plan in mind.

The Nudge

In late 2007, the same client and I met again. This time, I felt a clear nudge—a subtle but persistent prompting—that it was time to sell the firms. We agreed on an employment offer, and I began the transition process to occur around the start of 2008. The transition itself took several months to complete.

I know the Holy Spirit was the one nudging and directing me to sell.

The Timing

My employment with this client began approximately eighteen months before I received my dire cancer diagnosis. It was only one year after my final transition to full-time employment that I was enrolled in a new group health insurance plan.

The Miracle

This new insurance coverage ultimately saved us over $75,000 in medical costs. Even more remarkably, Mayo Clinic was listed as in-network under this health plan.

Connection

God was preparing me, financially and in many other ways, long before I truly needed the benefits of working for someone else. At the time, this career change seemed logical and timely. Looking back, it was providential.

The Diagnosis Change – July 23, 2009

Context

Eight pathology slides confirmed adenocarcinoma of the pancreas—the most lethal form of pancreatic cancer—with a life expectancy of less than one year. The cancer was also labeled poorly differentiated, indicating a more aggressive and fast-growing disease. (See Part III for full details.)

The Miracle

Just ten days later, I received a new diagnosis: pancreatic neuroendocrine tumor (pNET)—a much slower-growing and more treatable cancer. After surgery, my cancer was also classified as well differentiated, which is the complete opposite of poorly differentiated and carries a significantly better prognosis.

This was further proof of God's direct intervention—not only changing the cancer type, but also its biological behavior.

Medically

Both diagnoses were accurate at their respective times. I know this for a fact.

The Evidence

The Porter pathology report versus the University Hospital blood markers and imaging confirmed this progression.

Connection

God altered my cancer type. He was involved in the minutiae of my diagnosis—down to the cellular level.

The Life Verse – August 30, 2009

Context

Two weeks after the University Hospital diagnosis, and exactly two weeks before my surgery, I watched a sermon while at our cabin in the mountains.

The Moment

That day, I heard and claimed my life verse—my anchor: Isaiah 41:10.

The Timing

It came when I needed it, just two weeks before my difficult surgery and the long recovery that would follow.

Connection

God provided me with spiritual armor before the battle I was yet to face.

The Pre-Op Peace – September 15, 2009

Context

I was awaiting my turn for major surgery, surrounded by other patients who appeared far sicker than I was.

The Fragrance

While we waited in the pre-operative waiting room, we noticed the distinct scent of roses, often regarded as a sign of divine presence.

The Miracle

That day, while lying on the cold pre-op table, I focused intently on my life verse. I was overwhelmed by a supernatural peace that passed all comprehension.

Connection

God's presence was tangible in my moment of greatest vulnerability and fear, unlike any other medical procedure I had ever experienced.

The Wedding Ring – September 15, 2009

Context

My wedding ring was far too tight. There was no way I could remove it from my finger. We were told it might have to be cut off, which would destroy the ring.

The Miracle

The surgical team removed the ring intact, without any damage.

The Symbolism

Just as the ring was removed undamaged, my tumor was removed laparoscopically, without a bucket handle size surgical scar, our marriage would survive as well.

Connection

God was signaling healing that went beyond my physical body.

The Hospital Visitation (Day 11) – September 26, 2009 (Saturday)

Context

I was not improving. I was in severe pain, physically exhausted, and losing hope.

The Experience

At 1:00 a.m., Jesus appeared to me, accompanied by Mary.

His Words

"Today you will have a very rough day, but you will get better."

The Fulfillment

I nearly died that day—declared a Code Blue—after which my recovery began.

The Evidence

The doctor's chart note, written at 9:38 p.m. that evening, used the exact words: *"Rough day."*

Connection

God intervened at the precise moment when I was ready to give up.

The Mountain Prayer – 2011

Context

About a month earlier, I had been given a Stage IV diagnosis. The cancer had metastasized to my liver.

The Moment

While driving home from our cabin in the mountains, I prayed aloud, commanding, repeatedly, that my cancer leave me.

The Response

I was overwhelmed by a sense of warmth, accompanied by the Holy Spirit's reassurance: *"I will work on that."*

The Timeline

That prayer was answered ten years later.

Connection

God teaches us persistence in prayer.

"Be joyful in hope, patient in affliction, faithful in prayer." (Romans 12:12)

The Long Preservation – 2011–2016

Context

I was living with Stage IV pancreatic cancer, which carries a very low five-year survival rate since it had metastasized.

The Miracle

Five years of life with stable disease, despite a Stage IV diagnosis.

Medical Explanation

Aggressive treatment was required. However, many patients on the same or similar protocols did not fare as well. In many cases, chemotherapy causes more harm than benefit after approximately two years, particularly to bone marrow and overall blood health.

Connection

God sustained my life far beyond medical expectations.

Psalm 30:2, *"Lord my God, I called to you for help, and you healed me."*

The Liver Cleansing – February 2021

Context

I experienced several days during the month when I felt significantly unwell.

The Crisis

Blood tests revealed what was described as liver failure.

The Recovery

Within two days, follow-up blood tests returned to near-normal levels.

The Later Realization

In hindsight, God was cleansing my liver of cancer during the period when those blood tests reflected liver failure.

Connection

A physical healing that corresponded directly to my prayer in January 2021.

The Voice – June 2021

Context

I was awakened from my sleep.

The Message

"Ask your oncologist if you still have cancer."

The Specificity

Not a declaration of healing, but a clear instruction to seek confirmation through my oncologist.

Connection

God directed me to uncover the miracle through medical verification, which ultimately led to the biopsy.

The Benign Liver Biopsy – July 29, 2021

Context

The largest liver lesion was biopsied to either prove or deny the continued presence of cancer.

The Result

Benign — medically unexpected and, by standard clinical reasoning, improbable.

The Declaration

"I have been healed. I am cancer free."

Connection

The culmination of a twelve-year cancer journey, ten years living with Stage IV disease, and the fulfillment of my ten-year prayer.

Isaiah 25:1, *"LORD, you are my God; I will exalt you and praise your name, for in perfect faithfulness you have done wonderful things, things planned long ago!"*

The Aspen Tree Moment – 2011–2024

Context

Praying alone at our mountain cabin, amongst a stand of aspen trees.

The Response

As I finished praying, a sudden wind arose, causing the aspen leaves to quake and shimmer—followed by immediate and complete stillness.

The Message

A quiet but unmistakable sense that God was acknowledging my prayer.

Connection

One of many "small" miracles that demonstrated God's attention to detail and personal presence.

Illustration Note

The illustration included here is of an aspen tree that Kay drew. It closely resembles the tree which I was sitting beside on the day described above.

The Renewal Event – 2021

Context

Attending *The Renewal* conference in Florida, during a guided prayer exercise.

The Experience

A visualization in which Jesus came to me and gently removed burdens from the palm of my outstretched hand.

The Impact

A tangible sensation of peace and divine presence.

Connection

A continuation of, and further confirmation of, the consistent pattern of God's closeness to me, and to us.

Angel Visit and Angel References – Late April 1996

Context

While traveling to New Orleans, a taxi driver offered to wait while we checked into our accommodations. Upon arrival, he knew this area was unsafe.

The Intervention

After we confirmed the accommodations were not suitable and explained that everything else was booked due to a jazz festival weekend, the driver offered to find us a safe place to stay.

The Outcome

He drove us to a pleasant hotel late that day, which was closer to the areas we planned to visit. He stopped near the entrance and helped us unload our suitcases.

The Experience

We turned away briefly to pull out cash for a generous tip, but when we turned back, the cab driver was gone. We did not see his car leave, nor his tail lights.

We had the cab company name and the driver's name. The next day, we called to express our gratitude—only to discover that neither the cab company nor the driver existed.

The Impact

We believe God sent a guardian angel to protect us that night, guiding us to safety when we had nowhere else to go.

The Connection

We had always believed in guardian angels, but this was the first time we encountered one face to face. It was no coincidence he appeared at precisely the right moment.

- APPENDIX C -
BOOK'S NAMING

Book Name and Subtitle

I want to share how this book received its title and subtitle.

In mid-2025, while driving home and praying about this book, I began asking God what a fitting title for it should be. As I prayed, a phrase came clearly to my heart: *Holding My Hand.* I understood it to mean that God had always been there, always holding my hand, and that He would continue to do so forever. That phrase deeply resonated with and me and I knew it related to the message of this book.

Originally, the working title was Jesus Has, Is Now, and Forever Holding My Hand. Over time, however, it became clear that this phrase, while deeply personal, needed to be broadened to better reflect the full scope of the book's message. Eventually, the title evolved into *In the Hands of Our Heavenly Father,* which more fully captures the overarching theme of God's constant presence, guidance, and care.

My original title now became the foundation for the subtitle. My publisher suggested that the subtitle clearly convey the heart of my story healing, prayer, and hope. From that guidance, the subtitle became:

A True Story of Faith, Prayer, and Miraculous Healing from Stage IV Cancer

This subtitle remained unchanged, as it accurately and powerfully reflects the journey shared within these pages.

Throughout the book, I frequently use words and phrases such as *blessings, hope, holding my hand, miracles, and I could not imagine.* These words are not accidental; they form the emotional and spiritual thread woven throughout the entire narrative. They represent not only my experiences but also the truths I have come to know through them.

The original purpose of this book also changed as I continued writing. What began as a story focused primarily on my cancer journey gradually transformed into something much broader. It became a testimony of God's miraculous healing, His faithfulness, and the hope that comes from trusting Him fully. As the chapters unfolded, another theme became increasingly clear: how deeply and consistently God has been involved in my entire life, not just during my illness, but always.

Writing this book has drawn me closer to God in ways I never anticipated. That, in itself, has been a tremendous blessing. One I did not expect, yet one I treasure deeply.

This book is nothing short of a miracle in its own right. God was always there guiding, comforting, healing, and, indeed, holding my hand.

FAMILY LETTERS

From My Children

I asked each of my children to write something for me to include in this book. Several reviewers suggested that these letters were not directly relevant to the book's central themes of hope, being a cancer survivor, healing, or my journey. However, I felt it was important to include them, and they are shared below.

Some of the letters, much like Kay's chapters earlier in the book, reveal how my diagnosis affected those closest to me. They reflect their feelings, fears, and experiences during a frightening and uncertain time. I believe they add depth and perspective to the journey I was on, showing not only what I experienced, but also what my family endured alongside me.

You have no obligation to read these letters in order to understand my journey. However, I believe each one adds something meaningful to this book, both in revealing the impact my illness had on my children and in reflecting the person and father I was, and the man I have become.

Dad, from Daisy

My dad seems to be the one who has all the answers. And obviously, he would disagree with that statement. But it seems to me that whenever I have a question or need advice, he has the answer. If he does not, which is few and far between, he spends the next few days looking for it or offering me four additional options he didn't think of in the moment. He is my magic genie.

One of my earliest memories of my dad, for whatever reason, is him carrying me back across the hallway in the middle of the night. I would sneak into my parents' room after having a bad dream, trying not to wake him as I crawled across their bedroom floor toward my mom's side of the bed. Inevitably, I would end up in my dad's arms, walking back down that same hallway to be tucked back into my own bed. This memory probably sticks with me because it happened so many times during my childhood.

I would say my dad and I had a different relationship when I was younger than we do now. I don't think it was until high school or college that something shifted.

During my middle school and high school years, I participated in Westernaires. One of my most vivid memories with my dad is the countless early Saturday morning drives hauling the horse trailer, horses loaded, on our way to Westernaires events. One Saturday in particular stands out. We were listening to the radio when

Diamond Rio's "Meet in the Middle" came on. We both sang along, leaning our heads together over the console, quite literally "meeting in the middle."

From Westernaires, to college, to cowboy mounted shooting, and now to life on the farm, I have always felt supported by my dad. I'm sure he was just as supportive when I was younger, but as a child, it was harder to see and feel. You don't always recognize those things when you're young.

I am incredibly thankful to have the dad I have. To say more would take an entirely new book.

Dad, from Brian

Not many children can say that their dad chose them. But that is true for me. My dad chose to become my father. He adopted me when I was a small boy. I became a Zebarth, his son. I have no memory of life with any other father.

Over the decades that followed, my dad attended countless sports games and break-dance events, cheering me on through every stage of my life: the single years, marriage, and even my own journey into fatherhood. My dad is someone I can always count on to have my best interests at heart, to be in my corner, rooting for what is good, and for God's glory to shine through my life and the lives of my six children his grandchildren.

Then came the shock of all shocks.

In 2009, my dad told me he had pancreatic cancer. That news took the wind out of my sails. I felt helpless and overwhelmed, unsure of what I could possibly do to help. At the time, my family and I were halfway around the world in Brussels, Belgium. This was my dad, facing a dreadful disease, and I was so far away.

As a Christian, I knew the most important thing I could do was pray. As a family, we prayed for healing and wisdom, for every doctor and nurse, for my dad and Kay, for my brothers and sister, and for everyone who loved my dad. And so did countless others. My dad ran to the Lord, seeking healing and strength for each new trial. His church family prayed faithfully alongside him.

The Whipple surgery came with a long and difficult recovery. But after many months, Dad began receiving positive reports about the effectiveness of the surgery and treatments.

Today, it amazes me to see him as he is, playing volleyball in the yard, hunting Easter eggs with the grandkids, making delicious pumpkin pies and waffles, and telling the silly jokes we all love. Even more than that, it brings me great joy to see my dad give all the praise to God for His loving care, protection, and healing.

I love that our Heavenly Father is so good and gracious. He draws sinful people to Himself and gives them new life through His perfect Son. We do not have to earn it, it is a gift.

Just like my dad choosing to adopt me.

I could not earn his love or acceptance. I could do nothing on my own to become a Zebarth. But God had big plans for both of us. The healing given to my dad through doctors, nutrition, medical advancements, surgery, and treatments—is astonishing and causes my heart to rejoice and praise the Lord.

Back in 2009, when everything felt lost, we did not know God's plan. Now we can see it more clearly. My dad's days were far from over. God still had work for him to do here on earth. His light shines brightly through his deep love for his family and his Savior.

I am so blessed to be his son.

To God be the glory!!

He is risen — He is risen indeed!

Dad, from Zachary

A little while back, during a work meeting, some teammates and I were discussing mentoring and its importance in our lives. One question was posed to everyone: "Who would you say is the most important mentor in your life, and why?"

When it came my turn, I said something along the lines of, "I've had a lot of mentors throughout my life, and I've taken lessons from each of them. Those experiences have helped shape me into who I am today." While that statement wasn't untrue, upon reflection I realized it significantly undersold the influence of one person who has been my mentor for my entire life.

If I were asked that question again today, my answer would be unequivocal: my dad has been—and continues to be—my most important mentor, and there are countless reasons why.

Throughout my life, whenever I've been less than 100 percent certain about a decision, the person I've called to talk it through has been my dad. He has been a constant source of guidance in helping me navigate life's choices, both big and small. Whether it was major decisions like moving across the country for graduate school or changing (or not changing) jobs, or smaller but still important ones like enrolling in benefits or choosing a contractor, he has always been there. He listens patiently, offers thoughtful advice, shares from his deep well of experience, and provides steady, loving counsel.

Beyond advice, my dad's mentoring has come through his example. He has always led by example, consistently practicing what he preaches and living out his values. One trait that stands out most to me, and one I know he passed down, is his work ethic. I vividly remember growing up, back when he owned his own business, watching him work incredibly long hours, especially during tax season. There were countless late nights, early mornings, and weekends devoted to his clients, all in pursuit of building a successful business that could provide for our family.

The results of that hard work were evident. My sister and I never lacked for anything we needed, and we were blessed with opportunities to travel, explore the world, and participate in a wide range of extracurricular activities. Watching how my dad's dedication paid off, for him and for our family, was a form of mentoring in itself. It deeply shaped my own work ethic and my willingness to put in the time and effort required to succeed.

Connected to that is a piece of advice my dad gave me years ago that has stayed with me ever since: "You can survive anything for a period of time." He shared this maxim with me during moments when I needed it most. The length of time might vary, sometimes a month, sometimes several months, sometimes a year, but the message was always the same: there are seasons in life when you must endure something difficult to reach what lies on the other side.

My dad modeled this repeatedly, working through demanding stretches, persevering through long days and tough seasons: and seeing him do so proved to me that endurance was possible. It taught me that I could do the same. Whether it was long hours, difficult commutes, intense studying, challenging roommates, or difficult coworkers, I learned that pushing through those seasons would eventually bring reward. This lesson has been foundational in my life, helping me face challenges with grit and perseverance. Time and again, it has proven true: enduring those hardships has strengthened my career, my relationships, and my personal growth.

There's a common saying that we become who we are because of our parents. That can be true in both positive and negative ways—sometimes shaped by their successes, sometimes by their mistakes. Like any family, there were moments of struggle growing up, but those memories pale in comparison to the overwhelming positives. Without my dad's mentorship, there is no doubt I would be a very different person today. He has helped guide countless decisions that shaped my life and shown me, through his example, how to work hard, persevere through difficulty, and strive to be a better husband, professional, and human being.

It has now been fifteen years since my parents sat my sister and me down to tell us about my dad's cancer diagnosis. The fear and uncertainty of that moment, and the months and years that followed, are hard to put into words. At eighteen, I knew I still had so much growing left to do, and the possibility that my dad might not be there to continue guiding me was terrifying. I can't imagine where, or who, I would be today if that original prognosis had come true. I am profoundly grateful that I never had to find out.

These days, I don't reach out to my dad as often as I did when we first learned about his diagnosis. Part of that is likely because the fear of losing him no longer feels so immediate, making it easier to take our time together for granted. But I also believe something else is true: after years of his teaching, guidance, and example, his voice has become part of me.

All those years of calling him for advice, watching how he lives, and learning from his choices have shaped me so deeply that I often already know what he would say. His mentoring lives on within me. And yet, ever since that day fifteen years ago, every moment with my dad has felt like a gift—time and memories I once feared I might never have.

I don't want to take that for granted. I want to continue learning from his wisdom and experience as we both grow older. Ask me now who my most important mentor is, and my answer is clear: my dad. I feel incredibly blessed to have had such an extraordinary mentor for my entire life.

Dad, from Bill

At a very young age, I was told that my older sister and I were adopted. I never really understood what that meant until my younger brother was born. I remember my dad standing at the window, looking at my baby brother, and saying to me, "Well, now you have to grow up and be a big brother."

From that moment on, I felt lost. Being the middle child, I felt left out, like I no longer had a place. When I walked down the street and saw people, I wondered if any of them were my biological mom or dad. I didn't know what they looked like. I wondered what I would do if they lived nearby.

While I was in college, I decided it was time to look for my biological parents. I reached out to the Children's Home Aid Society, the adoption agency that had handled my adoption, and began the process. Not too long afterward, they told me, "We found your dad, and he's actually been looking for you too."

The emotions I felt in that moment were overwhelming excitement, nervousness, fear, amazement, all at once. After several phone calls, I learned that I also had a biological brother and sister. Then something incredible happened: my first job interview was in Denver, Colorado. I couldn't believe it. God worked in an amazing way to arrange that interview on the very day I would meet my biological dad for the first time.

When I stepped off the plane, he was standing at the gate. I looked at him and thought, That's him. We looked so much alike. Over time, through several trips, adventures, and countless shared experiences, snowmobiling, driving to Pikes Peak, playing card games, laser tag, and hiking through the woods, we got to know each other well.

Growing up, movies gave me a picture of a "dream dad" : someone who is always there for you, says the right things, does things with you, helps you through life, and makes everything better. That is my dad. He has been there through my marriage struggles and divorce, the adoption of my two kids, financial challenges, job changes you name it. He has always been there to listen.

So when I learned that my dad had cancer, my world turned upside down. The person who had always been so strong for me was now the one I needed to be strong for. I remember going to my quiet place and crying my eyes out.

God works in amazing ways. Shortly before my dad had his Whipple surgery, he was in Minnesota visiting the Mayo Clinic. At the same time, my employer flew me to Minneapolis for a week of work. I took that opportunity to meet Dad and Kay for dinner a gift I will always treasure.

Then came the dreaded call.

"Hey Bill. I've been told I won't make it for a year."

I knew it was possible, but I wasn't prepared for it, and I didn't want to believe it. I dropped everything to make sure I was in Denver for Christmas that year. The next day, we went to their cabin. We cried, talked for a long time, and tried to make sense of it all. How could this be happening?

That night, I prayed to God: Please don't take my dad. I need him in my life. I'm not ready for him to go.

Much later came the unbelievable call. My dad told me his cancer was gone, that he was finally off the medications and here we stand today.

We've had many long talks since then. He told me how much he wanted to be there to see Daisy get married and to see Zach graduate. He never lost faith. I struggled with mine at times, and he was always there to help bring me back through phone calls, encouragement, and by sharing his own experiences. Because of my dad, I have become a stronger Christian.

He was even in The Chosen television series. He's helped me with bathroom repairs and countless other projects. I treasure our nearly weekly phone calls and look forward to all that is still to come.

Love ya, Dad.

- APPENDIX E -
SUPPORTING MEDICAL DOCUMENTATION

Purpose of This Appendix

I have included selected medical records not to overwhelm the reader with medical jargon, but to demonstrate that the miracles described in this book are well documented. The diagnosis change, the benign biopsy, and my long-term survival with Stage IV cancer are not faith claims alone, they are supported by objective medical records.

These documents are included to show that my testimony is grounded in verifiable facts, not merely personal belief. Each document is summarized and annotated to highlight its significance within my cancer journey.

Key Medical Documents

Document 1: Porter Hospital Pathology Report

Date: July 23, 2009

Description: Pathology report showing diagnosis of adenocarcinoma.

Name: Dan R Zebarth | DOB: 1/14/1952 | MRN: 1828847 | PCP: ███████████████ | Legal Name: Daniel R Zebarth

General Pathology Report

Collected on Aug 04, 2009 2:40 PM

Mayo Clinic

Results

08/04/2009 Path Review of Outside Specimen (HR09-40622)

Referring Physician:
██████████████████

Porter Adventist Hospital
2525 South Downing Street
Denver, CO 80210
303-778-5786
Requested By: ████████████████████████

DIAGNOSIS:
Pancreas, uncinate mass, endoscopic fine needle aspiration
(EN09-194; 7/23/2009): Positive for malignancy. Poorly
differentiated malignant neoplasm, favor adenocarcinoma.

Seen in consultation with ██████████████████

8/5/2009 14:49 Interpreted by: ████████████████████
Report electronically signed by ██████████████████████
Transcribed by: jmp22 8/5/2009 14:27:42

SPECIMEN DESCRIPTION:
A:Cytology Consultation

TISSUE DESCRIPTION:

MATERIAL RECEIVED:
FNA pancreas - 8 slides (EN09-194), 1 CD
SLIDE DISPOSITION:
1 CD sent to Dr. J. Clain on 8/5/09 - jmp
8 slides returned 8/12/09 - jmp

Authorizing provider: ██████████████████████
Collection date: Aug 04, 2009 2:40 PM
Result date: Aug 04, 2009 2:40 PM

Result status: Final
Resulting lab:
MAYO CLINIC LABORATORIES - ROCHESTER MAIN CAMPUS
200 First Street SW
Rochester MN 55905
████████████████████ (Lab director)

Key Findings:

- Eight tissue slides examined

- Confirmed poorly differentiated adenocarcinoma

- Aggressive cancer classification

Annotation:

"This diagnosis represented a medical death sentence at the time, with an expected survival of approximately 8–12 months."

Document 2: University Hospital Blood Work

Date: August 3, 2009

Description: Blood work showing markers consistent with a pancreatic neuroendocrine tumor (pNET), including elevated Chromogranin A.

Name: Dan R Zebarth | DOB: 1/14/1952 | MRN: 1828847 | PCP: ▮▮▮▮▮▮▮▮▮▮ | Legal Name: Daniel R Zebarth

CHROMOGRANIN A

Collected on Aug 06, 2009 11:00 AM

Results

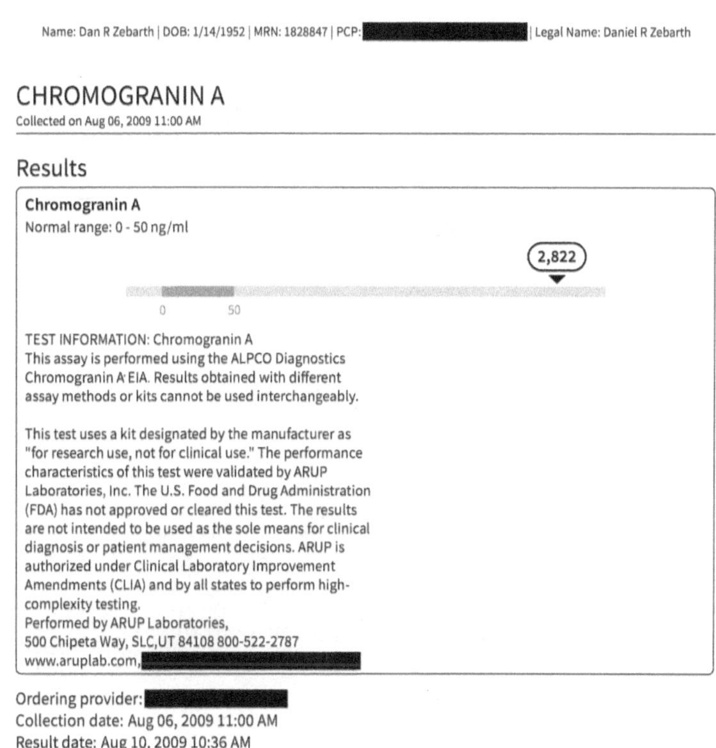

Chromogranin A
Normal range: 0 - 50 ng/ml

2,822

0   50

TEST INFORMATION: Chromogranin A
This assay is performed using the ALPCO Diagnostics
Chromogranin A EIA. Results obtained with different
assay methods or kits cannot be used interchangeably.

This test uses a kit designated by the manufacturer as
"for research use, not for clinical use." The performance
characteristics of this test were validated by ARUP
Laboratories, Inc. The U.S. Food and Drug Administration
(FDA) has not approved or cleared this test. The results
are not intended to be used as the sole means for clinical
diagnosis or patient management decisions. ARUP is
authorized under Clinical Laboratory Improvement
Amendments (CLIA) and by all states to perform high-
complexity testing.
Performed by ARUP Laboratories,
500 Chipeta Way, SLC,UT 84108 800-522-2787
www.aruplab.com, ▮▮▮▮▮▮▮▮▮▮▮▮

Ordering provider: ▮▮▮▮▮▮▮▮
Collection date: Aug 06, 2009 11:00 AM
Result date: Aug 10, 2009 10:36 AM
Result status: Final
Resulting lab:
CERNER

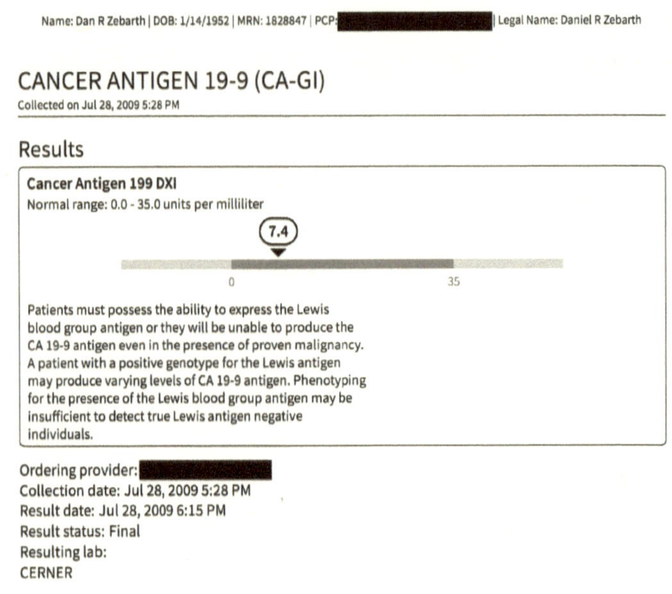

Name: Dan R Zebarth | DOB: 1/14/1952 | MRN: 1828847 | PCP: ███████████████ | Legal Name: Daniel R Zebarth

CANCER ANTIGEN 19-9 (CA-GI)

Collected on Jul 28, 2009 5:28 PM

Results

Cancer Antigen 199 DXI

Normal range: 0.0 - 35.0 units per milliliter

7.4

0   35

Patients must possess the ability to express the Lewis blood group antigen or they will be unable to produce the CA 19-9 antigen even in the presence of proven malignancy. A patient with a positive genotype for the Lewis antigen may produce varying levels of CA 19-9 antigen. Phenotyping for the presence of the Lewis blood group antigen may be insufficient to detect true Lewis antigen negative individuals.

Ordering provider: ███████████████
Collection date: Jul 28, 2009 5:28 PM
Result date: Jul 28, 2009 6:15 PM
Result status: Final
Resulting lab:
CERNER

MyChart® licensed from Epic Systems Corporation© 1999 - 2025

Key Findings:

- Different cancer type identified just ten days after the Porter report

- Findings inconsistent with adenocarcinoma

Annotation:

"Two distinct diagnoses within ten days. Both reports were medically accurate at the time they were rendered. I believe God changed the cancer itself."

Document 3: Mayo Clinic Surgical Pathology

Date: September 18, 2009

Description: Final surgical pathology following Whipple procedure.

Mr. Daniel R. Zebarth
Summary of Care, generated on Jun. 06, 2023

Service Date/Time: 18-Sep-2009 11:58
Provider: █████████████████████████ Pager: 8-2865
Service: ONCLCI Type/Desc: LE Status: Fnl Revision #: 2

REFERRAL
████████████████████████████████

CHIEF COMPLAINT/PURPOSE OF VISIT
Treatment recommendations following resection of node negative pancreatic islet cell tumor.

Collaborating physician, ███████████

HISTORY OF PRESENT ILLNESS
Mr. Zebarth is a pleasant 57-year-old gentleman from Littleton, CO. We are seeing him at the request of ████████ surgical service to discuss treatment recommendations following resection of his node negative pancreatic islet cell tumor. His history is as follows.

1. July 10, 2009, due to abdominal pain and pressure, underwent an ultrasound to rule out gallstones. This procedure noted a 2.8 x 2.9 x 3.3 cm solid mass in the uncinate process of the pancreatic head. He was also noted to have small hepatic cysts and the common bile duct was mildly dilated (8 mm). Subsequent CT scan confirming the mass within the head of the pancreas. Also noting low attenuated lesion in the posterior segment of the right hepatic lobe measuring approximately 7 cm in size.
2. July 23, 2009, EUS with fine needle aspirate performed by his local provider again documenting a 2.7 cm mass in the uncinate process of the pancreas. Fine needle aspirate read out at home with poorly differentiated malignancy. This pathology was reviewed here at Mayo Clinic and found to be positive for malignancy, poorly differentiated malignant neoplasm favor adenocarcinoma.
3. Patient was subsequently evaluated at the University of Colorado suspecting that this was an islet cell tumor. At that time, blood tests included normal gastrin level (22) and serotonin (115). Noted to have a elevated chromogranin A at 2822 with normal being 0-50. Ultrasound was performed at that facility of the liver which noted a suspicious lesion that was not biopsied.
4. August 18, 2009, presented to Mayo Clinic for evaluation. Ultrasound again of the liver noting a 1.3 x 1.3 x 1.1 cm mass in the right lobe of the liver. This was biopsied and smear was negative for malignancy. Tissue was positive for cavernous hemangioma.
5. September 14, 2009, CT scan performed at Mayo Clinic of the abdomen noting a 3.5 cm well marginated pancreatic head mass. This second mass appears to be abutting the proximal portal vein. Imaging is characteristic suggestive of an islet cell tumor. Patient noted to have a 1 cm lymph node anterior to the pancreatic mass. Multiple low density lesions throughout the liver. Tiny indeterminate pulmonary nodule on the right lower lobe.
6. September 15, 2009, █████████████ performed a laparoscopic pylorus preserving pancreaticoduodenectomy en-bloc with tangential excision of the superior mesenteric vein. Also performed a cholecystectomy. Per operative report, exploration demonstrated no growth abnormalities of the visible peritoneum or visceral surfaces. In the head of the pancreas was a large mass without evidence of unresectability. There appeared to be tumor involvement of the posterolateral aspect of the superior mesenteric vein near the insertion of the ileocolonic vein. Further evaluation noted that the ileocolonic vein also had what appeared to be a tumor thrombus within it where a pancreatic venus tributary entered. Based on those findings a tangential excision of the superior mesenteric vein to include the segment of the ileocolonic vein was performed. Original uncinate margin was positive. Additional margin was obtained with no gross visible tumor. Pathology of the Whipple tissue was positive for well-differentiated endocrine tumor of uncertain behavior (WHO 1b) forming a 5.0 x 3.5 x 3.0 cm mass. Neoplastic cells are strongly positive for CK19, CAM 5.2, chromogranin, and synaptophysin. The tumor is infiltrative and confined to the pancreas. Vascular invasion is present. Necrosis and increased mitosis are absent. The resected margins are negative for tumor including the uncinate and portal vein groove margins after reexcision of the uncinate margin. Sixteen lymph nodes negative for tumor. Gallbladder is cystologically unremarkable. Two superior mesenteric artery, one common hepatic, and one right gastric artery lymph node biopsy, all negative for metastatic disease.

Today, Mr. Zebarth is three days postoperative. He is alert and oriented and able to carry on a very good discussion. His wife is present during this consultation.

REVIEWED INFORMATION WITH PATIENT AS NOTED ON THE CURRENT VISIT INFORMATION FORM, DATED 17-Aug-2009 AND ON THE PATIENT FAMILY HISTORY FORM, DATED 17-Aug-2009.

CURRENT MEDICATIONS
Emergen-C® (Free Text Entry) 1 packet by mouth one time daily.

Flaxseed Oil capsule 1 capsule by mouth two times a day.
Instructions: 1 gram.

Glucosamine-Chondroitin tablet 2 tablets by mouth one time daily.
Instructions: 1500/800.

MoviPrep 100-7.5-2.691 gram powder in packet 2,000 mL by mouth once.
Instructions: Procedures before noon: Evening-before regimen at 6 PM & 1 1/2 hrs after finishing 6 PM dose on day prior. Procedures at or after Noon: split dose regimen at 6 PM day prior and 7 AM day of procedure.

Multivitamin tablet 1 tablet by mouth one time daily.

Muro 128 drops 2 drops ophthalmic as directed by prescriber.
Site: Both eyes.
Instructions: one to two times in the AM.

Ropinirole 0.5 mg tablet 1 tablet by mouth every evening.

Vitamin C 500 mg tablet 1 tablet by mouth every morning.

These are the patient's medications as of Tuesday, September 15, 2009 at 9:24 AM.

Key Findings:

- Confirmed pancreatic neuroendocrine tumor (pNET)

- 25 lymph nodes examined – all negative

- Clean surgical margins

- No evidence of any cancer remaining

Annotation:

"Final confirmation that the cancer was pNET, not adenocarcinoma. This dramatically altered prognosis and treatment."

Document 4: ICU Physician Chart Note – Dr. T. Dominguez

Date: September 26, 2009

Description: ICU progress note written following a medical crisis.

Formatting of this note might be different from the original.
DEMOGRAPHIC INFORMATION:
Clinic Number: 7-086-964
Patient Name: Mr. Daniel R. Zebarth
Age: 57 Y
Birthdate: 14-Jan-1952 Sex: M
Address: 7568 South Storm Mountain City: Littleton, CO 80127-3807

Service Date/Time: 26-Sep-2009 09:38
Provider: ███████████ Pager:
Service: SKENDI Type/Desc: PROG Status: Fnl Revision #: 1

PHYSICAL EXAM:
Abdomen: On exam, his abdomen is very soft. It is mildly distended and mildly tender. All of his incisions are healing well. Does have some mild edema in his lower extremities.

ASSESSMENT / PLAN:
Mr. Zebarth had an excellent day yesterday. However, this morning he started having severe crampy abdominal pain as well as nausea. He is passing gas and having bowel movements now. His vital signs remain normal, and he has remained afebrile. Percutaneous drain continues to drain very little amounts. His laboratory analysis was remarkable for leukocytosis which increased from 20,000 to 21,000 this morning. His electrolytes are normal.

Today will administer some suppositories to try to stimulate his bowel function further and encourage the passage of flatus. Will continue intravenous anticoagulation with heparin. Will partially back out his drain in anticipation for removal of the drain tomorrow.

Original: dac/kmg
Electronically Signed: 26-Sep-2009 19:18 ███████████

Clinical Notes - DOC02600 Id: 1383953214 Status: Fnl

Electronically signed by Rst C at 03/11/2018 2:30 PM CDT

Plan of Treatment - documented as of this encounter
Not on file

Results - documented in this encounter
ECG - Final result (09/26/2009 4:40 PM CDT)

Specimen (Source)	Anatomical Location / Laterality	Collection Method / Volume	Collection Time	Received Time
			09/26/2009 4:40 PM CDT	

Narrative

Authorizing Provider	Result Type
Historical Provider	ECG ORDERABLES

Performing Organization	Address	City/State/ZIP Code	Phone Number
FOUNDATION RADIOLOGY SYSTEM	1979 Milky Way	Madison, WI 53593, USA	

Mr. Daniel R. Zebarth
Summary of Care, generated on Jun. 06, 2023

Progress Notes - documented in this encounter
▮▮▮▮▮▮▮▮▮▮▮▮▮▮▮ - 09/26/2009 7:36 PM CDT
Formatting of this note might be different from the original.
DEMOGRAPHIC INFORMATION:
Clinic Number: 7-086-964
Patient Name: Mr. Daniel R. Zebarth
Age: 57 Y
Birthdate: 14-Jan-1952 Sex: M
Address: 7568 South Storm Mountain City: Littleton, CO 80127-3807

Service Date/Time: 26-Sep-2009 19:36
Provider: ▮▮▮▮▮▮▮▮▮▮▮▮▮▮▮▮▮▮▮▮▮
Service: SKENDI Type/Desc: PROG Status: Fnl Revision #: 2

REVISION HISTORY:
Sep-26-2009 20:22:42 - Modification to Service, SUBJECTIVE by ▮▮▮▮▮▮▮▮▮▮▮

SUBJECTIVE:
Mr Zebarth has been having a rough day. Since this morning he's been complaining of crampy abdominal pain and nausea. Around 3:30 pm he had an episode of hematemesis approx 300 ml of digested blood. Subsequently he had a syncope episode. His blood pressure was 68/45 and HR 108. A 1000 ml bolus of normal saline was started and he responded well, his BP came back to 122/67.

Excerpt:

"9:38 PM – Mr. Zebarth is having a rough day."

Annotation:

"Final confirmation that the cancer was pNET, not adenocarcinoma. This dramatically altered prognosis and treatment."

Document 5: Stage IV Diagnosis Imaging

Date: June 2011

Description: MRI imaging revealing metastatic lesions in the liver.

Clinical Notes - DOC00641 Id: 384974023 Status: Fnl

Name: Daniel R. Zebarth | DOB: 1/14/1952 | MRN: 7-086-964 | PCP:

RST Conversion Encounter - Jun 16, 2011

with ████████████ at Hx Rst No Mapping

Notes from Care Team

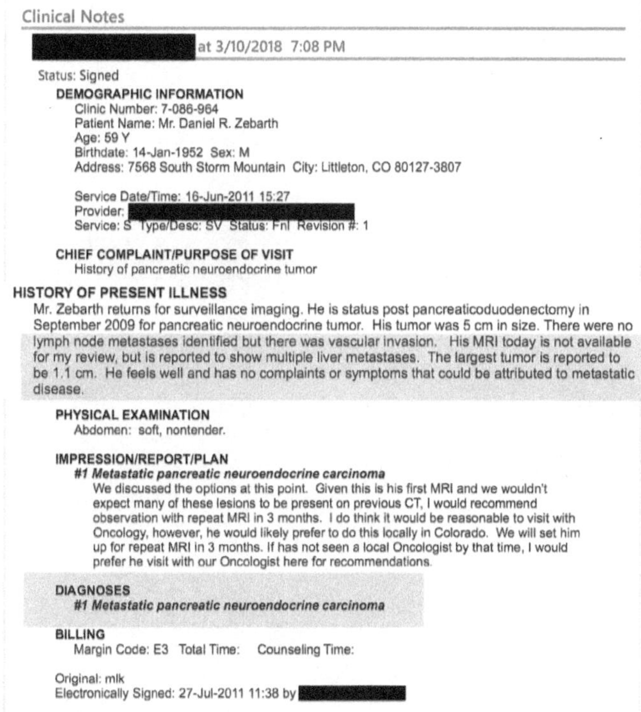

Clinical Notes

████████████ at 3/10/2018 7:08 PM

Status: Signed

DEMOGRAPHIC INFORMATION
Clinic Number: 7-086-964
Patient Name: Mr. Daniel R. Zebarth
Age: 59 Y
Birthdate: 14-Jan-1952 Sex: M
Address: 7568 South Storm Mountain City: Littleton, CO 80127-3807

Service Date/Time: 16-Jun-2011 15:27
Provider: ████████████
Service: S Type/Desc: SV Status: Fnl Revision #: 1

CHIEF COMPLAINT/PURPOSE OF VISIT
History of pancreatic neuroendocrine tumor

HISTORY OF PRESENT ILLNESS
Mr. Zebarth returns for surveillance imaging. He is status post pancreaticoduodenectomy in September 2009 for pancreatic neuroendocrine tumor. His tumor was 5 cm in size. There were no lymph node metastases identified but there was vascular invasion. His MRI today is not available for my review, but is reported to show multiple liver metastases. The largest tumor is reported to be 1.1 cm. He feels well and has no complaints or symptoms that could be attributed to metastatic disease.

PHYSICAL EXAMINATION
Abdomen: soft, nontender.

IMPRESSION/REPORT/PLAN
#1 Metastatic pancreatic neuroendocrine carcinoma
We discussed the options at this point. Given this is his first MRI and we wouldn't expect many of these lesions to be present on previous CT, I would recommend observation with repeat MRI in 3 months. I do think it would be reasonable to visit with Oncology, however, he would likely prefer to do this locally in Colorado. We will set him up for repeat MRI in 3 months. If has not seen a local Oncologist by that time, I would prefer he visit with our Oncologist here for recommendations.

DIAGNOSES
#1 Metastatic pancreatic neuroendocrine carcinoma

BILLING
Margin Code: E3 Total Time: Counseling Time:

Original: mlk
Electronically Signed: 27-Jul-2011 11:38 by ████████████

Key Findings:

- Multiple liver lesions consistent with metastatic disease

- Diagnosis: Stage IV pancreatic neuroendocrine cancer

Annotation:

"Stage IV disease. At the time, five-year survival rates were estimated at approximately 19%."

Document 6: DOTATATE PET Scan

Date: June 6, 2018

Description: PET scan confirming active neuroendocrine cancer in the liver.

Impression

IMPRESSION:

1. Two discrete radiotracer avid central mesenteric nodes compatible with metastasis.

2. Asymmetric increased uptake in the left adrenal nonspecific however due to the degree of asymmetry and underlying metastasis cannot be excluded. Attention follow-up imaging for a developing nodule increasing asymmetry is recommended.

3. Multiple hepatic metastasis in the left and right lobes redemonstrated.

4. Radiotracer uptake in a right thyroid nodule which is grossly unchanged in size when compared to 2015. Recommend further evaluation with dedicated thyroid ultrasound.

If you are a health care provider and have any questions regarding this or any other Nuclear Medicine report please call: (720) 848 - 7209. The Nuclear Medicine reading room location is: OP-1504 AOP. We are staffed 8 AM to 5 PM Monday through Friday. For urgent matters after hours or on weekends please call (720) 848 - 8666.

If you are a patient and have questions about your report please contact your health care provider.

Report E-Signed By: ████████████ at 6/7/2018 8:55 AM

WSN:PACSR62749

Narrative

68Ga-DOTATATE PET-CT STANDARD

DATE OF SERVICE: 06/06/2018, 1658

INDICATION: Evaluate for neural endocrine tumor prior to PRRT. Initial treatment strategy.

COMPARISON: CT chest 4/2/2018

RADIOPHARMACEUTICAL: 4.3 mCi Ga-68 DOTATATE IV

PROCEDURE: 62 minutes after IV radiotracer administration via a right chest port vein, positron emission tomography was performed from the base of the skull to the proximal thighs. Noncontrast helical CT imaging was performed over the same range without breath-hold for attenuation correction of PET images and anatomic correlation, but not for primary interpretation as it is not of standard diagnostic quality. CT images were reconstructed in the axial, coronal and sagittal views. Fusion images and a maximal intensity projection (MIP) image were also generated.

FINDINGS:

HEAD AND NECK: No radiotracer avid lymphadenopathy in the head or neck.

Subcentimeter thyroid nodule in the right gland with SUV max of 2.8 (image 57). This is grossly stable in size when compared to 2/12/2015.

CHEST: No radiotracer avid mediastinal or hilar lymphadenopathy. No suspicious pulmonary nodules.

ABDOMEN AND PELVIS: Multiple radiotracer avid hypodense hepatic metastasis throughout the left and right hepatic lobes are redemonstrated. For example, metastasis in hepatic segment III demonstrates SUV max of 31 and measures approximately 1.5 cm, grossly stable in size when compared to MR on 4/2/2018 (image 126). The largest metastasis in the inferior right lobe, bilobed, measures up to 6.1 cm with SUV max of 95 (image 143) this is also not significantly changed in size compared to prior MR.

Soft tissue density in the central mesenteric fat adjacent to a surgical clip is unchanged in size measuring up to 1.8 centimeter. There is an adjacent focus of increased radiotracer uptake with SUV max of 72 (image 151).

A second soft tissue density slightly more superiorly measures up to 1.5 cm (image 153). A second focus of increased radiotracer uptake nearby demonstrates SUV max of 27.1 without clear correlate on CT (image 149). These findings are favored to represent misregistration.

Asymmetric increased radiotracer uptake in the left greater than right adrenal gland with SUV max on the left measuring 15.8 (image 134).

Intense radiotracer uptake in the region of the gastric fundus is likely physiologic. Status post Whipple procedure with plastic pancreatic duct stent in place.

MUSCULOSKELETAL: No radiotracer avid or destructive bone lesion. Physiologic uptake within the musculature.

Authorizing provider: █████████████████
Reading physician: ██████████████
Study date: Jun 06, 2018 4:58 PM
Collection date: Jun 07, 2018 8:01 AM
Result date: Jun 07, 2018 8:55 AM
Result status: Final

Key Findings:

- Persistent cancer presence nine years after original diagnosis

Annotation:

"Confirms that cancer was still present years after surgery, reinforcing that my later healing was not spontaneous remission from surgery alone."

Document 7: Liver Failure Laboratory Results

Date: February 2021

Description: Blood work showing acute liver dysfunction.

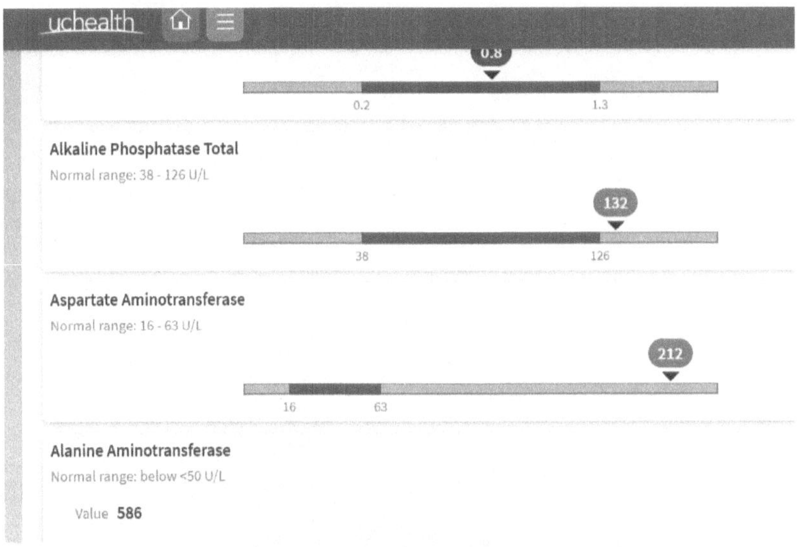

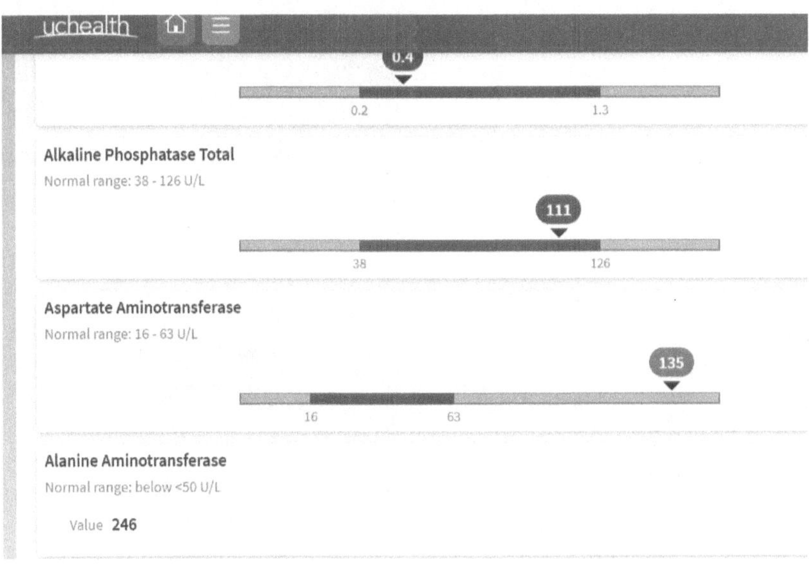

Key Findings:

- Significantly elevated liver enzymes

- Follow-up blood work 48 hours later showed near-normal values

Annotation:

"What appeared to be liver failure resolved rapidly. I believe this was the moment God cleansed my liver of cancer—what looked like dying was actually healing."

Document 8: Liver Lesion Biopsy – Benign

Date: July 27, 2021

Description: Pathology report from biopsy of largest liver lesion.

Name: Dan R Zebarth | DOB: 1/14/1952 | MRN: 1828847 | PCP: ▮▮▮▮▮▮▮▮▮▮▮

NON GYN CYTOLOGY REQUEST - Details

Study Result

Narrative

Highlands Ranch Hospital
1500 Park Central Drive
Highlands Ranch, CO 80129
Tel:720-516-0198 Fax:720-516-0222
Cytology Report

Clinical History
Metastatic pancreatic neuroendocrine tumor.

Final Cytologic Diagnosis
A. Liver mass, IR-guided core needle biopsy:
- Benign liver parenchyma with area of fibrosis.
- Negtive for metastatic tumor (see comment).

Comment
Patient's history of metastatic pancreatic neuroendocrine tumor is noted. However, no definitive evidence of tumor is identified in this biopsy specimen (confirmed with synaptophysin immunostain). Focal large bile duct structures are seen, which may correspond to the atypical cells seen on the touch prep at the onsite evaluation.

Final Diagnosis Reviewed and Interpreted By
▮▮▮▮▮▮▮▮▮▮
Electronically Signed, 7/29/2021

Key Findings:

- Lesion determined to be **benign**

- No evidence of malignancy

Annotation:

"The largest and most concerning lesion was biopsied and found to be benign. Medically unexpected given my history. For me, this marked the confirmation of divine healing."

Document 9: Overall Medical Review by UCH

Date: January 10, 2017

Description: Progress Notes - Reflective of oncologic history, chemotherapy to date

Reference: Documentation of Cancer journey through January 2017

Name: Dan R Zebarth | DOB: 1/14/1952 | MRN: 1828847 | PCP: █████████████ | Legal Name: Daniel R Zebarth

Office Visit - Jan 10, 2017

with Wells Messersmith, MD at UCHealth Cancer Care Clinic - Lone Tree

Notes from Care Team

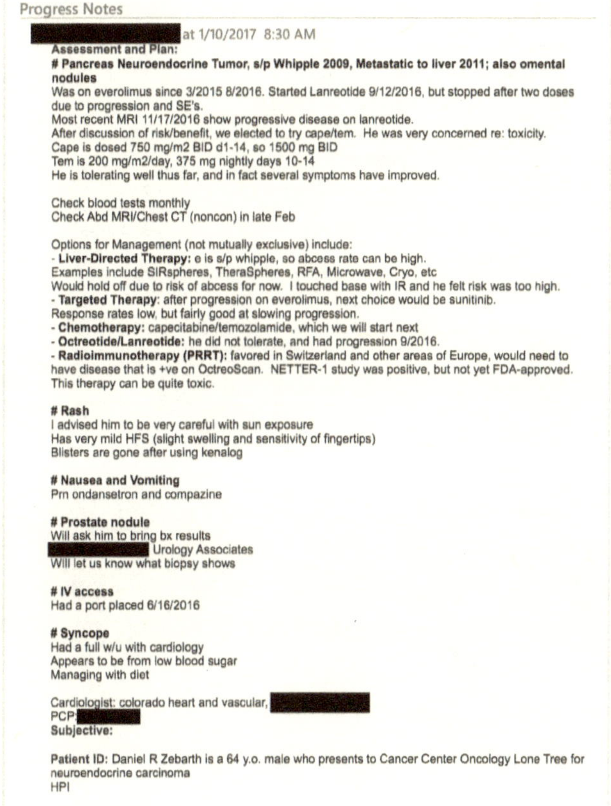

Progress Notes

█████████ at 1/10/2017 8:30 AM

Assessment and Plan:

 # Pancreas Neuroendocrine Tumor, s/p Whipple 2009, Metastatic to liver 2011; also omental nodules

Was on everolimus since 3/2015 8/2016. Started Lanreotide 9/12/2016, but stopped after two doses due to progression and SE's.

Most recent MRI 11/17/2016 show progressive disease on lanreotide.

After discussion of risk/benefit, we elected to try cape/tem. He was very concerned re: toxicity.

Cape is dosed 750 mg/m2 BID d1-14, so 1500 mg BID

Tem is 200 mg/m2/day, 375 mg nightly days 10-14

He is tolerating well thus far, and in fact several symptoms have improved.

Check blood tests monthly

Check Abd MRI/Chest CT (noncon) in late Feb

Options for Management (not mutually exclusive) include:
- **Liver-Directed Therapy:** e is s/p whipple, so abcess rate can be high.
Examples include SIRspheres, TheraSpheres, RFA, Microwave, Cryo, etc
Would hold off due to risk of abcess for now. I touched base with IR and he felt risk was too high.
- **Targeted Therapy:** after progression on everolimus, next choice would be sunitinib.
Response rates low, but fairly good at slowing progression.
- **Chemotherapy:** capecitabine/temozolamide, which we will start next
- **Octreotide/Lanreotide:** he did not tolerate, and had progression 9/2016.
- **Radioimmunotherapy (PRRT):** favored in Switzerland and other areas of Europe, would need to have disease that is +ve on OctreoScan. NETTER-1 study was positive, but not yet FDA-approved. This therapy can be quite toxic.

 # Rash
I advised him to be very careful with sun exposure
Has very mild HFS (slight swelling and sensitivity of fingertips)
Blisters are gone after using kenalog

 # Nausea and Vomiting
Prn ondansetron and compazine

 # Prostate nodule
Will ask him to bring bx results
█████████████ Urology Associates
Will let us know what biopsy shows

 # IV access
Had a port placed 6/16/2016

 # Syncope
Had a full w/u with cardiology
Appears to be from low blood sugar
Managing with diet

Cardiologist: colorado heart and vascular, ████████████
PCP: ██████
Subjective:

Patient ID: Daniel R Zebarth is a 64 y.o. male who presents to Cancer Center Oncology Lone Tree for neuroendocrine carcinoma
HPI

Since he was last seen, he has been doing OK
Had some blisters between fingers after using eucerin, his wife had the same thing
Started on kenalog
Several things have improved since starting chemo
No longer having low blood sugars; ankle swelling gone; finger joint pain is gone
Having some sensitivity to sun (forehead, nose)

Has had some intermittent RUQ pain, lasts a few minutes
Does have fatigue, sleeping a but more
Had a few episodes of n/v
Not much diarrhea

Resting HR in the high 40's/low 50's, seems to be his new baseline
Eyes are fine
No flushing
No palps

ONCOLOGIC HISTORY
1. In July 2009, p/w epigastric pain, abd u/s showed 2.9 cm mass in head of pancreas; CT showed same, and ?R liver lobe mass.
July 23,2009 underwent FNA of panc mass; indeterminate (adenoCA versus islet cell tumor); had elevated chromogranin A
Seen at Mayo Clinic August 2009. Bx of R lobe of liver showed hemangioma. CT showed 3.5 cm panc mass; also liver cysts
2. Underwent lap Whipple at Mayo by ▮▮▮▮▮▮ on 9/15/2009. No evidence of distant spread during surgery.
Surg path showed 5 cm panc neuroendocrine tumor, neg margins, 0/20 LN's involved.
Then underwent surveillance regularly.
3. Was disease free until 2/2011 (~18m), had indeterminate liver lesions. In June of 2011, MRI repeated and showed new liver lesions. Repeat imaging at 3m shows now change. Annual MRI's in 2012, 2013, and 4/2014 showed slowly progressive disease. MRI 11/2014 showed increasing tumor burden.
4. Started everolimus (Afinitor) 10mg 3/2/15, held for mucositis 3/23/15. Restarted at 2.5 mg daily -> 5mg daily.
D/c'd 8/30/2016 due to progression.
5. Started lanreotide 9/12/2016; dose #2 on 10/13/2016. course c/b bradycardia/syncope.
MRI abd showed progression 11/17/2016.
6. Started cape/tem c1d1 on 12/27/2016. Developed contact dermatitis (not HFS) on 1/4/2017, started on kenalog.

PAST MEDICAL HISTORY:
#Pancreas neuroendocrine tumor as above, metastatic to liver
#Patient has a history of 3 kidney stones in the past.
#Hernia was repaired at Swedish on 10/17/2014, tolerated well
One umbulical, bilateral inguinal hernia repairs by ▮▮▮▮▮
#Mild Meniuere's dz (occaisonal dizziness; sensitivty to loud noise)
#Fuchs corneal dystrophy; s/p Descemet's Stripping Automated Endothelial Keratoplasty (DSAEK) 5/4/2015 (R) and 8/3/2015 (L)
Harvard Park Surgery Center; ▮▮▮▮▮
#Had an injection of his L knee after being diagnosed with left iliotibial band friction syndrome
#Low blood sugars leading to syncope in Fall 2016. Was all the way down to 47.
Cardiac w/u negative (echo, holter, etc).

He eats mostly a vegan diet and avoids sugars. He has dropped about 20# since 2009 on purpose.

PAST SURGICAL HISTORY:
He had a tonsillectomy as a child, umbilical hernia repair in 2003 and a lithotripsy.

SH
Has lived her in Colorado for 30yr, from midwest
Here with wife Kay; 1 boy and 1 girl (UIC PT school; Metro state)
Works as a CFO
Likes to hike
No tob, No illicits

FH
Mother, 59, pulmonary embolus
Father, 59, stomach cancer
3 sisters, age 75 and up
Middle sister has DM, osteoarthritis
Otherwise fairly healthy

CURRENT MEDICATIONS:
Current Outpatient Prescriptions

FINDINGS:

ABDOMEN:

Liver: Numerous enhancing lesions are noted throughout the liver, predominantly in the right hepatic lobe which are consistent with neuroendocrine metastases. Several T1 hypointense lesions are also noted and compatible with cysts, others are indeterminate. Evaluation is difficult due to the number of lesions however overall there is a more confluent appearance and all reference lesions appear larger. Reference lesions discussed below:

-Larger segment 5/6 lesion measures 34 x 30 mm(image 41 series 5), 30 x 26 mm previously, (previously 29 x 26 mm on prior and 28 x 20 mm earlier)
-Larger segment 7 lesion now measures 38 x 30 mm (image 23 series 5) , 34 x 28 mm previously, (previously 27 x 25 mm on prior and 21 x 28 mm earlier)
-Larger segment 7/8 lesion now measures 34 x 33 mm (image 21 series 5), 33 x 26 mm previously, (previously 24 x 23 mm on prior and 21 x 21 mm earlier). This lesion appears confluent with the adjacent 52 x 35 hepatic segment 7/6 lesion (image 15 series 5) that previously measured 40 x 28 mm, and earlier 38 x 26 mm.

Bile ducts: Stable extrahepatic common bile duct prominence most likely related to postcholecystectomy changes.

Gallbladder: Surgically absent.

Pancreas: 3 mm T2 hyperintensity in the pancreatic tail is stable and indeterminate (series 12 image 12). Postsurgical changes of Whipple procedure with stable mild prominence of the main pancreatic duct secondary to the pancreaticojejunostomy.

Spleen: The spleen is normal

Kidneys: Multiple T2 hyperintensities are scattered throughout the kidneys, predominantly on the right. Dominant cyst in the lower pole of the right kidney is stable. Additional lesions are too small to characterize, these are likely benign and are unchanged. Incidental left retroaortic renal vein

Adrenals: Normal.

GI tract: Postsurgical changes of Whipple procedure. The bowel is nondilated. The midline mesenteric nodule now measures 27 mm (series 5 image 55), previously 24 mm. Slightly more superior 19 mm implant (series 5, image 47) is also slightly enlarged, previously 17 mm.

PELVIS:

Urinary Bladder: There is no significant wall thickening or focal mass.

Reproductive organs: Mildly enlarged prostate.

Rectum and Anus: Normal

No ascites.

Lung bases are clear. Heterogeneous bone marrow in the pelvis probably represents osteopenia. Degenerative spondylosis along the vertebral column.

TIME/COUNSELING:
I personally spent a total of 45 minutes. Of that 25 minutes was counseling/coordination of patient's care. See my note above for details.

Closing Reflections

These documents are not presented to argue theology, but to demonstrate that **faith and documented medical reality can coexist.** My healing is not explained by a single treatment, test, or coincidence. It unfolded over time, through medicine, prayer, perseverance, and what I believe was the supernatural intervention of God.

This appendix exists so that readers—believers and skeptics alike—can see that my testimony is anchored in evidence, not imagination.

Medical Term Glossary

Adenocarcinoma (of the Pancreas)

A common and highly aggressive form of pancreatic cancer that arises from the glandular cells of the pancreas. It is often diagnosed at an advanced stage and historically carries a poor prognosis, with limited long-term survival rates.

pNET (Pancreatic Neuroendocrine Tumor)

A rarer type of pancreatic cancer that originates in the hormone-producing (neuroendocrine) cells of the pancreas. pNETs are often slower growing than adenocarcinoma and may respond to different treatments, sometimes allowing for longer survival.

Chromogranin A (CgA)

A blood test that measures a protein released by neuroendocrine cells. It is commonly used as a tumor marker to help diagnose, monitor, and track disease progression or response to treatment in patients with neuroendocrine tumors, including pNETs.

Stage IV / Metastasis

Both terms indicate that cancer has spread from its original location to distant organs or tissues (such as the liver). Stage IV cancer is considered advanced and typically not curable by surgery alone, though it may be managed with treatment.

Whipple Procedure (Pancreaticoduodenectomy)

A major and complex surgical operation used primarily to treat pancreatic cancer. It involves removal of the head of the pancreas, gallbladder, part of the bile duct, the duodenum (first part of the small intestine), and sometimes a portion of the stomach. The digestive system is then reconstructed. Recovery is significant and may require long-term enzyme replacement or insulin therapy.

Lesion

A general medical term for an abnormal area of tissue. In the liver, lesions may represent cysts, benign growths, or tumors (either benign or cancerous). Further testing is often required to determine their nature.

Benign vs. Malignant

- **Benign:** Non-cancerous growths that typically grow slowly, remain localized, and do not spread to other parts of the body.

- **Malignant:** Cancerous growths that can grow rapidly, invade nearby tissues, and spread (metastasize) to distant organs through the bloodstream or lymphatic system, making them potentially life-threatening.

REFERENCES
& RESOURCES

The following books, authors, and resources influenced my thinking, faith, and understanding during my cancer journey. Some are medical, some spiritual, and others deeply personal. Together, they reflect the wide range of perspectives that shaped my hope, resilience, and trust in God.

90 Minutes in Heaven
Don Piper
Published 2004

The Healing Light
Agnes Sanford
Published 1963

The China Study
T. Colin Campbell, PhD, and Thomas M. Campbell, MD

Heaven Is for Real
Todd Burpo and Lynn Vincent
Published 2010

Healing Prayer on Holy Ground
Mark Sheehan, MD, with Chris Sheehan
Published 2010

The Messianic Church Arising
Robert D. Heidler, PhD
Published 2006; revised edition 2011

Touching Heaven
Chauncey Crandall, MD
Published 2016

HEALINGS CONTINUE

Here are two miracle stories that demonstrate that God is still working in our time.

Richard B. Whitaker

Prairie Times, October 2024 (Article Summary)

My wife discovered a lump. Her mother had passed away from breast cancer just a few years earlier. After several tests, the doctor called to say the mass was cancerous. A wave of numbness flooded over her, like a tsunami rolling in from the sea.

As she told me the news, unable to speak, I formed these words in my mind:

"Oh Heavenly Father, please do not take her from me now. Please, Father."

I repeated this prayer more than once.

Suddenly, I felt an overwhelming warmth flow through my body, from my head to my toes, followed by a profound sense of peace.

A few days before surgery, I placed my hands on her head and relied on the Holy Spirit to place words in my mind—words that a loving Heavenly Father would want her to hear. She knew, with sufficient faith and prayers offered, that the operation would be successful.

She believed God promised her total recovery and a return to excellent health. She also sensed that the Lord still had more for her to accomplish.

As time passed, after surgery and chemotherapy, her ability and desire to share her remarkable story increased. She never hesitated to talk with others about her healing journey, which included her faith in God and the power of friends and family.

More than twenty-six years have passed since her surgery. Today, she is the matriarch of a family with seven children, twenty-one grandchildren, and ten great-grandchildren. For her, faith in God, coupled with a positive mental attitude and a desire to serve others, resulted in many years of being cancer-free.

Yes, faith preceded the miracle.

Epoch News

October 4, 2024

A fifty-eight-year-old man was diagnosed with Stage IV cancer that had spread to 90 percent of his bones. He was given three months to live.

He had been feeling exhausted and in pain, which he initially dismissed. As his symptoms worsened, he went to the emergency room, where doctors delivered the life-changing diagnosis: Stage IV cancer that had metastasized to his bones and lymph nodes. He was told to go home and be with his family and was placed in hospice care.

Then something extraordinary happened.

The room suddenly turned cold for no apparent reason. He looked up and saw someone standing in front of him. That person stepped forward, reached out, and touched him on the shoulder. In that moment, he heard the words: *"You are in the presence of Jesus."*

He had not been to church in ten years and was confused by the experience. The encounter lasted only seconds, but it changed the course of his life. He felt an overwhelming sense of peace and knew he was going to make it through. He continued to hear a voice saying, *"You are going to make it through this."*

That touch of divine presence fueled his determination to fight cancer.

He went through six rounds of chemotherapy. Despite his positive mindset, the treatment took a heavy toll. He hated chemotherapy, but he refused to let it sideline him completely. He said he endured chemo because it was what his doctors recommended, believing it was part of his journey and one that would later allow him to relate to and coach others facing similar battles.

Six months after starting treatment, he returned to the hospital for another scan. The results stunned his oncologist.

"My doctor had studied cancer all over the world and had never seen anything like this," he said. The doctor told him, *"This is not medicine. It is miraculous."*

The cancer that had invaded his bones was completely gone. Not only had the cancer disappeared, but his bones—once riddled with disease—had healed so completely that doctors could hardly believe they had ever been damaged.

The healing was nothing short of divine intervention.

God had cured him. It changed everything. His faith, once shaken, was now firm again.

Today, he travels the world sharing his story of hope and healing through the **Living Hope Cancer Foundation,** which offers free coaching and support to cancer patients and their families. He believes in miracles.

The foundation's motto is:
"Get Up and Live."

Please Share Your Story

If God has worked in your life through healing, hope, or restoration, I would love to hear from you.
Dan Zebarth
Cell / Text: **303-918-5002**
Email: **dzebarth@msn.com**

CREDITS

Chris Sheehan

I owe much to Chris Sheehan, my editor, who helped immensely with editing and with thoughtful suggestions on how to improve my early manuscripts.

In 2014, I had an appointment at South Denver Cardiology. When I entered their medical clinic, I noticed a placard displaying information about a book entitled *Healing Prayer on Holy Ground,* by Mark Sheehan, MD, a cardiologist, with Chris Sheehan. The book immediately caught my interest, and I made a point to purchase it. Both Kay and I read it.

Fast forward to 2024.

Kay and a longtime friend of hers, who lives in our neighborhood, went for a walk to catch up, as they had not seen each other in quite some time. During their conversation, her friend shared that she had met someone while playing pickleball. As she described her new friend, she mentioned that he was a writer and that he had written a book with his dad on healing prayer.

Kay instantly recognized the book we had read nearly ten years earlier and wondered aloud whether Chris might be able to help me finish my manuscript. I had reached a point where I knew I needed professional advice and guidance.

When Kay returned from the walk, she excitedly told me about this remarkable discovery. We reached out to Chris, and he graciously agreed to help me with my book.

I marvel at the orchestration of these details across our lives—the connections, the individuals, and the timing. It is both encouraging and reassuring to see how God is working. He knows us intimately, and He cares about us and loves us deeply.

Thank you, Chris, for your time, your help with editing, and your thoughtful feedback on the early versions of this book. I still well up with emotion when I think back to your first series of comments and encouragement.

You were, and are, a Godsend.

Spirit Media Publishing

Spirit Media Publishing, the publisher we chose for this book, has an amazing team.

I submitted my manuscript to approximately twelve Christian-based publishers. About half of them accepted the manuscript and were willing to work with me. I quickly narrowed that list down to three.

There were many reasons why Kay and I chose Spirit Media, but three stood out above the rest:

1. They are Kingdom-of-God focused, specializing in personal stories that serve as testimonies and glorify God and His amazing goodness and love.

2. They actually read my manuscript and provided an extensive evaluation called a *Manuscript Review*, which genuinely brought me to tears.

3. The deciding factor: Kevin, the founder and CEO of Spirit Media Publishing, offered to pray over our decision regarding which publisher we should choose. His unbiased prayer convinced us that Spirit Media was the right choice.

As we moved through the process of editing, designing the front and back covers, and formatting the book, their willingness to work within our desired timeline was deeply appreciated. We worked closely with David in client relations, Lisa in editing, and of course, Kevin. We also know there were many others working behind the scenes who were instrumental in bringing this final product to life.

Thank you, Kevin, and your entire team, for the extensive time you spent providing thoughtful input and meaningful feedback—including help with chapter titles, more concise wording, and so much more. Your professional knowledge and talent helped bring my story into the world so that others may have hope and a deeper awareness of the goodness of our Heavenly Father.

Thank you all so very much.

—Daniel Zebarth

CASTLEWOOD CANYON CHURCH

A PLACE WHERE WORSHIP COMES ALIVE

A Church centered on Yeshua and guided by the Spirit

Scan the QR code
to learn more

www.ccanyonc.org

IN THE
HANDS OF
OUR
HEAVENLY
FATHER

A True Story of
Faith, Prayer, and
Miraculous
Healing from
Cancer

ANIEL ZE

https://inhisheavenlyhands.wixsite.com/inhishands